THE PREACHER AND HIS MODELS

THE

PREACHER AND HIS MODELS

THE YALE LECTURES ON PREACHING, 1891.

BY THE REV.

JAMES STALKER, D.D.,

AUTHOR OF

"THE LIFE OF JESUS CHRIST," "THE LIFE OF ST. PAUL," ETC.

Solid Ground Christian Books
Birmingham, Alabama

SOLID GROUND CHRISTIAN BOOKS
PO Box 660132, Vestavia Hills, AL 35266
205-443-0311
sgcb@charter.net
http://www.solid-ground-books.com

The Preacher and His Models

by James Stalker (1848-1927)

Taken from the 1892 edition by Hodder & Stoughton

Published by Solid Ground Christian Books

Classic Reprints Series

First printing November 2003

ISBN: 1-932474-16-1

Manufactured in the United States of America

PREFACE.

THESE nine Lectures on Preaching were delivered, on the Lyman Beecher Foundation, to the divinity students of Yale University in the spring of this year. With the kind concurrence of the Senate of Yale, five of them were redelivered, on the Merrick Foundation, to the students of Delaware University, Ohio.

In the Appendix an Ordination Address is reproduced, which I wrote when I had been only four or five years in the ministry, and which I have been requested to reprint. My friend, the Rev. Dr. Walker, who was present when it was delivered, having published it in *The Family Treasury*, another friend, noticing it there, had it printed as a pamphlet at his own expense and distributed to all the ministers of the Church to which he and I belong. It was a very characteristic act; and I have ventured, as a memorial of it, to dedicate this volume to him. I do so, however, not for this reason only, but also because there has been no one in this generation who has done more than he has done, by the example of his own impressive ministry and by his generous encouragement of younger ministers, to promote the interests of preaching in his native land.

My thanks are due to the Rev. Charles Shaw, who on this as on former occasions has kindly assisted me in correcting the press.

GLASGOW, *October* 1*st*, 1891.

PREFACE

TO THE SECOND EDITION.

THE publishers inform me, that in a few weeks they have disposed of an edition of five thousand copies, and that a new edition is required. I have no alterations to make beyond a few verbal corrections. In connection with the ninth lecture, on the intellectual work of the ministry, I may be allowed to refer to an article contributed to the *Expositor*, April, 1890, on *The Present Desiderata of Theology*, in which I have endeavoured to indicate the departments of study which most deserve the attention of those who wish to keep abreast of the times or to do original work.

CONTENTS.

LECTURE I.

LECTURE I.

INTRODUCTORY

LECTURE I.

INTRODUCTORY.

GENTLEMEN, it would be impossible to begin this course of lectures without expressing my acknowledgments to the Theological Faculty of this University for the great honour they have done me by inviting me to occupy this position. When I look over the list of my predecessors and observe that it includes such names as Henry Ward Beecher, Dr. John Hall, Dr. W. M. Taylor, Dr. Phillips Brooks and Dr. Dale—to mention only those with which it opens—I cannot help feeling that it is perhaps a greater honour than I was entitled to accept; and I cannot but wish that the preaching of the old country were to be represented on this occasion by some one of the many ministers who would have been abler than I to do it justice. It is with no sense of having attained that I am to speak to you; for I always seem to myself to be only beginning to learn my trade; and the furthest I ever get in the way of confidence is to believe that I shall preach well next

time. However, there may be some advantages in
hearing one who is not too far away from the difficulties with which you will soon be contending
yourselves ; and the keenness with which I have felt
these difficulties may have made me reflect, more than
others to whom the path of excellence has been
easier, on the means of overcoming them.

I warmly reciprocate the sentiments which have led
the Faculty to come across the Atlantic the second
time for a lecturer, and the liberality of mind with
which they are wont to overstep the boundaries of
their own denomination and select their lecturers
from all the evangelical Churches. It is the first time
I have set foot on your continent, but I have long
entertained a warm admiration for the American
people and a firm faith in their destiny ; and I
welcome an opportunity which may serve, in any
degree, to demonstrate the unity which underlies the
variety of our evangelical communions, and to show
how great are the things in which we agree in comparison with those on which we differ.

The aim of this lectureship, if I have apprehended
it aright, is that men who are out on the sea of
practical life, feeling the force and strain of the winds
and currents of the time, and who therefore occupy,
to some extent, a different point of view from either

students or professors, should come and tell you, who are still standing on the *terra firma* of college life, but will soon also have to launch forth on the same element, how it feels out there on the deep.

Well, there is a considerable difference.

The professorial theory of college life is, that the faculties are being exercised and the resources collected with which the battles of life are subsequently to be fought and its victories won. And there is, no doubt, a great deal of truth in this theory. The acquisitions of the class-room will all be found useful in future, and your only regret will be that they have not been more extensive and thorough. The gymnastic of study is suppling faculties which will be indispensable hereafter. Yet there is room amidst your studies, and without the slightest disparagement to them, for a message more directly from life, to hint to you, that more may be needed in the career to which you are looking forward than a college can give, and that the powers on which success in practical life depends may be somewhat different from those which avail most at your present stage.

There are two very marked types of intellect to be observed amongst men, which we may call the receptive and the creative. Receptive intellect has the power of taking fully in what is addressed to it by others. It separates its acquisitions and distributes

them among the pigeon-holes of the memory. Out
of these again it can reproduce them, as occasion
requires, and even make what may be called permu-
tations and combinations among its materials with
skill and facility. The creative intellect, on the
contrary, is sometimes anything but apt to receive
that which people attempt to put into it. Instead
of being an open, roomy vessel for holding things,
it may be awkwardly shaped, and sometimes difficult
to open at all. Nor do things pour out of it in a
stream, as water does from a pitcher ; they rather
flash out of it, like sparks from the anvil. Instead of
possessing its own knowledge, it is possessed by it ; it
burns as it emits it, and its fire is contagious.

The former is the serviceable intellect at college,
but it is the latter which makes the preacher. There
may, indeed, here and there, be miraculous professors
who attach more importance, and give higher marks,
to the indications of the creative intellect than to the
achievements of the receptive intellect. But few can
resist the appeal made by the clear, correct and
copious reproduction of what they have themselves
supplied. Indeed, they would not, as a rule, be
justified in doing so ; for the first indications of
originality are often crude and irritating, and they
may come to nothing. · The creative intellect is frequently slow in maturing; it is like those seeds which

take more than one season to blossom. But at a flower show it would not be fair to withhold the prize from the flower which has blossomed already, and reserve it for one which may possibly do so next year.

Of my fellow-students in the class to which I belonged at college, the two who have since been most successful did not then seem destined for first places. They were known to be able men, but they were not excessively laborious, and they kept themselves irritatingly detached from the interests of the college. But the one has since unfolded a remarkable originality, which was, no doubt, even then organizing itself in the inner depths; and the other, as soon as he entered the pulpit, turned out to have the power of casting a spell over the minds of men. Both had a spark of nature's fire; and this is the possession which outshines all others when college is over and practical life begun.*

---

* " A set o' dull, conceited hashes
Confuse their brains in college classes,
They gang in stirks, and come out asses,
    Plain truth to speak,
An' syne they hope to speel Parnassus
    By dint o' Greek.

" Gi'e me *a'e spark o' nature's fire*,
That's a' the learnin' I desire,
Then, though I trudge through dub an' mire,
    At pleuch or cart,
My muse, though homely in attire,
    May touch the heart."— BURNS.

But, if the viewpoint of practical life is different even from the professorial, it is still more different from that of students ; and this may again justify the bringing of a message from the outside world. The difference might be put in many ways ; but perhaps it may be best expressed by saying, that, while you are among the critics, we are among the criticized.

In the history of nearly all minds of the better sort there is an epoch of criticism. The young soul, as it begins to observe, discovers that things around it are not all as they ought to be, and that the world is not so perfect a place as might naturally be expected or as it may have been represented to be. The critical faculty awakes and, having once tasted blood, rushes forth to judge all men and things with cruel ability. This is the stage at which we agree with Carlyle in thinking mankind to be mostly fools and pronounce every man over five-and-forty who does not happen to agree with our opinions an old fogey. It is the time when we are confident that we could, if we chose, single-handed and with ease, accomplish tasks which generations of men have struggled with in vain. Only in the meantime we, for our part, are not disposed to commit ourselves to any creed or to champion any cause, because we are engaged in contemplating all.

This period occurs, I say, in the history of all men of the abler sort ; but in students, on account of their peculiar opportunities, the symptoms are generally exceptionally pronounced. Students are the chartered libertines of criticism. What a life professors would lead, if they only knew what is said about them every day of their lives! I often think that three-fourths of every faculty in the country would disappear some morning by a simultaneous act of self-effacement. Of course ministers do not escape ; ecclesiastics and Church courts are quite beyond redemption ; and principalities and powers in general are in the same condemnation.

Such is the delightful prerogative of the position in which you now stand. But, gentlemen, the moment you leave these college gates behind, you have to pass from your place among the critics and take your place among the criticized. That is, you will have to quit the well-cushioned benches, where the spectators sit enjoying the spectacle, and take your place among the gladiators in the arena. The binoculars of the community will be turned upon you, and five hundred or a thousand people will be entitled to say twice or thrice every week what they think of your performances. You will have to put your shoulder under the huge mass of your Church's policy and try to keep step with some thousands whose shoulders are under it too ; and the reproaches cast by the public and the press at the awkwardness of the whole

squad and the unsteadiness of the ark will fall on
you along with the rest.

Seriously, this is a tremendous difference. Criticism,
however brilliant, is a comparatively easy thing. It
is easier to criticize the greatest things superbly than
to do even small things fairly well. A brief experience of practical life gives one a great respect
for some men whom one would not at one time
have considered very brilliant, and for work which
one would have pronounced very imperfect. There
is a famous passage in Lucretius, in which he speaks
of the joy of the mariner who has escaped to dry
land, when he sees his shipwrecked companions still
struggling in the waves. This is too heathenish a
sentiment; but I confess I have sometimes experienced
a touch of it, when I have beheld one who has distinguished himself by his incisiveness while still on
the *terra firma* of criticism, suddenly dropped into
the bottomless sea of actual life, and learning, amidst
his first struggles in the waves, not without gulps
of salt-water, the difference between intention and
performance.

But, gentlemen, do not suppose that I am persuad-
ing you to give up criticism. On the contrary, this
is the natural function of the stage at which you
are ; and probably those who throw themselves most

vigorously into it now may also discharge most successfully the functions of the stages yet to come. The world reaps not a little advantage from criticism. It is a very imperfect world; no generation of its inhabitants does its work as well as it ought to be done, and it is the undoubted right of the next generation to detect its defects ; for in this lies the only chance of improvement. There is something awe-inspiring in the first glance cast by the young on the world in which they find themselves. It is so clear and unbiassed ; they distinguish so instantaneously between the right and the wrong, the noble and the base ; and they blurt out so frankly what they see. As we grow older, we train ourselves unawares not to see straight or, if we see, we hold our peace. The first open look of young eyes on the condition of the world is one of the principal regenerative forces of humanity.

To begin with, therefore, at all events I will rather come to your standpoint than ask you to come to mine. Indeed, although I have for some time been among the criticized, and my sympathies are with the practical workers, my sense of how imperfectly the work is done, and of how inadequate our efforts are to the magnitude of the task, grows stronger instead of weaker. And it is from this point of view that I mean to enter into our subject. I will make use of the facts of my own country, with which I am familiar; but I do not suppose that the state of things among you is substantially different ; and you will not have much difficulty in correcting the picture, to make it correspond with your circumstances, whilst I speak.

In the present century there has certainly been an unparalleled multiplication of the instrumentalities for doing the work. The machine of religion, so to speak, has been perfected. The population has been increasing fast ; but churches have multiplied at least twice as fast. Even in a great city like Glasgow we have a Protestant church to every two thousand of the population.* And, inside the churches, the multiplication of agencies has been even more surprising. Formerly the minister did almost all the work ; and it comprehended little more than the two services on Sunday and the visitation of the congregation ; the elders helping him to a small extent in financing the congregation and in a few other matters largely secular. But now every congregation is a perfect hive of Christian activity. In a large

* On this side of the water it will be read with interest that " in 1880 there was in the United States one Evangelical Church organization to every 516 of the population. In Boston there is 1 church to every 1,600 of the population ; in Chicago 1 to 2,081 ; in New York 1 to 2,468 ; in St. Louis 1 to 2,800."—*Our Country*, by Rev. Josiah Strong, D.D.

congregation the workers are counted by hundreds. Every imaginable form of philanthropic and religious appliance is in operation. Buildings for Sabbath Schools and Mission Work are added to the church ; and nearly every day of the week has its meeting.

The machine of religion is large and complicated, and it is manned by so many workers that they get in each other's way; but, with all this bustling activity, is the work done ? This is the question which gives us pause. Has the amount of practical Christianity increased in proportion to the multiplication of agencies ? Are the prospects of religion as much brighter than they used to be as might have been expected after all this expenditure of labour ? Is Christianity deepening as well as spreading ?

In Glasgow, where the proportion of churches to population is so high, they speak of two hundred thousand non-church-goers, that is, a third of the inhabitants ; and, if you go into one of our villages with a population of two or three thousand, you may find three or four churches, belonging to different denominations ; but you will usually find even there a considerable body of non-church-goers. Not long ago I heard a London clergyman state, that if, any Sunday morning, you went through the congregations belonging to the Church of England in the district of a hundred and fifty thousand inhabitants in which he labours, you would not, in all of them put together, find one man present for every thousand of the population. One of the English bishops recently admitted that in South London his Church is not in possession ; and certainly no other denomination is. Thus, with all our appliances, we have failed even to bring the population within the sound of the Gospel.

Inside the churches, what is to be said ? Is the proportion large of those who have received the Gospel in such a way that their hearts have manifestly been changed by it and their lives brought under its sway ? We should utterly deceive ourselves if we imagined that real Christianity is co-extensive with the profession of Christianity. Many who bear the Christian name have neither Christian experience nor Christian character, but in their spirit and pursuits are thoroughly worldly. Even where religion has taken real hold, is the type very often beautiful and impressive ? Who can think without shame of the long delay of the Church even to attempt the work of converting the heathen ? And even yet the sacrifices made for this object are ludicrously small in proportion either to the magnitude of the problem or the wealth of the Christian community. The annual expenditure of the United Kingdom on drink is said to be a hundred times as great as that on foreign missions.

Religion does not permeate life. The Church is one of the great institutions of the country, and gets its own place. But it is a thing apart from the common life, which goes on beside it. Business, politics, literature, amusements, are only faintly coloured by it. Yet the mission of Christianity is not to occupy a respectable place apart, but to leaven life through and through.

Vice flourishes side by side with religion. We build the school and the church, and then we open beside them the public-house. The Christian community has the power of controlling this traffic ; but it allows it to go on with all its unspeakable horrors. Thus its own work is systematically undone, and faster than the victims can be saved new ones are manufactured to occupy their places. Of vices which are still more degrading I need not speak. Their prevalence is too patent everywhere. If there is any law of Christianity which is obvious and inexorable, it is the law of purity. But go where you will in the Christian countries, and you will learn that by large sections of their manhood this law is treated as if it did not exist. The truth is that, in spite of the nations being baptized in the name of Christ, heathenism has still the control of much of their life ; and it would hardly be too much to say that the mission of Christianity is still only beginning.

In what direction does hope lie? It seems to me that there can be no more important factor in the solution of the problem than the kind of men who fill the office of the ministry. We must have men of more power, more concentration on the aims of the ministry, more wisdom, but, above all, more willingness to sacrifice their lives to their vocation. We have too tame and conventional a way of thinking about our career. Men are not even ambitious of doing more than settling in a comfortable position and getting through its duties in a respectable way. We need to have men penetrated with the problem as a whole, and labouring with the new developments which the times require. The prizes of the ministry ought to be its posts of greatest difficulty. When a student or young minister proves to have the genuine gift, his natural goal should not be a highly paid place in a West End church, but a position where he would be in the forefront of the battle with sin and misery. Nowhere else are the great lines of Chapman more applicable than in our calling :—

> Give me a spirit that on this life's rough sea
> Loves to have his sails filled with a lusty wind,
> Even till his sailyards tremble, his masts crack,
> And his rapt ship runs on her side so low
> That she drinks water and her keel ploughs air.

I am well aware that men of this stamp cannot be

made to order. They must, as I have suggested already, have a spark of nature's fire, and, besides that, the Spirit of God must descend on them. Yet I have thought that it might be helpful towards this end to go back to the origins of preaching, and to study those in whom its primitive spirit was embodied. Perhaps that which we are desiderating could not be better expressed than by saying that we need a ministry prophetic and apostolic. And I am going to invite you to study the prophets and apostles as our models.

Though we may not believe in apostolic succession in the churchly sense, we are the successors of the apostles in this sense, that the apostles filled the office which we hold, or hope to hold, and illustrated the manner in which its duties should be discharged in such a way as to be an example and an inspiration to all its subsequent occupants. The air they breathed was still charged with the spirit poured into it by Christ ; they were made great by the influence of His teaching and companionship ; the power of the Holy Ghost, freshly descended, burned on their hearts ; and they went forth on their mission with a force of conviction and a mastery of their task which nothing could resist.

One among them embodied in himself, above all others, the spirit of that epoch of creative energy.

St. Paul is perhaps, after our Lord Himself, the most complete embodiment of the ministerial life on all its sides which the world has ever seen. And, fortunately, he embodied this spirit not only in deeds, but also in words. Circumstances made him a writer of letters, the most autobiographical form of literature. His friends, such as Timothy and Titus, drew out of him lengthy expressions of the convictions wrought into his mind by the experiences of a lifetime. His enemies, by their accusations, struck out of him still ampler and more heartfelt statements of his feelings and motives. St. Paul has painted his own portrait at full length, and in every line it is the portrait of a minister. There is more in his writings which touches the very quick of our life as ministers than in all other writings in existence. It is my desire to reproduce this straight from the sources. I have no intention of going over the outward life of St. Paul. This you can find in a hundred books. But I desire to exhibit the very soul of the man, as he himself has revealed it to us in his writings.

If we are the successors of the apostles, the apostles were the successors of the prophets, who did for the Church of the Old Testament what the apostles did for that of the New. In outward aspect and detail, indeed, the life of the prophets differed much from that of the apostles. In force of manhood and in variety and brilliance of genius they far excelled them. But their aim was the same. It was to make the kingdom of God come by announcing and enforcing the mind and will of God. And this is our aim too.

The writings of the prophets are very difficult, and their period is less popularly known than any other period of Scripture history, either before or after it. But it is beginning to attract more attention, and in the near future it will do so much more, because it is beginning to be perceived that in it lies the key to the whole Old Testament history and literature.* The writings of Isaiah especially have of late attracted attention. Commentary after commentary on them has appeared ;† till now the reader can see his way pretty clearly through the tangled but enchanting mazes of his writings. With such helps as have been available to me I have endeavoured through the writings to get at the man; and I will take Isaiah as the representative of the prophetic spirit in the same way as St. Paul is to represent for us the apostles. But here again my aim is neither that of the commentator nor that of the biographer. It is the soul of the man I wish to depict and the spirit of his work.

---

* See Duhm : *Die Theologie der Propheten*—Preface.
† Cheyne, Smith, Delitzsch, von Orelli, Dillmann, etc.

It may be thought that, by taking up the subject in this way, I am missing the opportunity of dealing with the practical work of to-day. But I do not think so. There are, indeed, some details nearly always discussed in lectures on preaching which I do not care to touch. There is, for instance, the question of the delivery of sermons—whether the preacher should read, or speak *memoriter*, or preach *extempore*. This can be discussed endlessly, and the discussion is always interesting ; but, if it were discussed every year for a century, it would be as far from being settled as ever. Besides, it is my duty to remember what others have handled exhaustively here before me. Indeed, the Senate mentioned to me that it was desirable that the subject should be taken up from a new point of view. They have been good enough to express their approbation of the way in which I mean to treat it ; but it is not in deference to their instructions that I take it up in this way, but in accordance with the bent of my own mind ; and I think I see my way to bring to bear on it all the practical experience which I may be in possession of ; for I quite recognise that the value of such a course of lectures largely depends on its being, from beginning to end, what in literature is called a Confession, that is, a record of experiences. Although I am to go back to the ages of the apostles and the prophets, I do not intend to stay there. My wish is to bring down from thence fire which will kindle your hearts, as you face the world and the tasks of to-day.

There is another objection, which may have already occurred to some of you, and would doubtless occur to many, as I went along, if I did not anticipate it. It may be felt, that both apostles and prophets were so differently situated from us, especially through the possession of the gift of inspiration, that they can be no example for us to follow. To this I will not reply by seeking in any way to minimise their inspiration. It is, indeed, difficult to say exactly how their inspiration differed from that which is accessible and indispensable to us ; for we also are entirely dependent for the power and success of our work on the same Spirit as spoke through them. But, however difficult it may be to define it, I am one of those who believe that there is a difference, and that it is a great difference. The mind and will of God expressed themselves through the prophets and apostles with a directness and authority which we cannot claim. But the difference is not such as to remove them beyond our imitation. Although in some, or even many, respects they may be beyond us, this is no reason why we may not in others imitate them with the greatest advantage. It will be seen at a glance how little there is in this objection, if it be considered that our Lord Himself

is the great pattern of the ministry.   In some respects
He is of course much farther away from us than either
prophets or apostles ; yet He is near us as a model in
every detail of our duty.   No mode of treating my
subject would have been so congenial to me as to set
Him forth in this character.   But, having attempted
to do so elsewhere, I have chosen the method now
announced under the conviction, that the nearest
approach to the study of how Christ fulfilled the duties
of the ministry is to study how prophets and apostles
fulfilled them.

There is one thing more which I should like to
say before closing this somewhat miscellaneous in-
troductory lecture.   I would not have come to lecture
to you on this subject if I were not a firm believer in
preaching.   If in what has been already said I have
seemed to depreciate its results, this is only because
my ideal is so high of what the pulpit ought to do,
and might do.*   I do not, indeed, separate preaching

---

* " After eleven years of active preaching I have spent five of hardly
less active hearing.   I have listened carefully to preachers of all degrees
and denominations, and some convictions have been burned in upon
my mind.   Far above all, I have learned to believe in the great importance of preaching—the effect it has on men's lives and thoughts ; their
need of it ; their pain and loss when it does not help and reach them.
I used to think that, if it did men good, they would speak more of it.
But they pay no compliments to their daily bread ; yet it is the stuff

from the other parts of a minister's life, such as the conducting of the service of the sanctuary, the visitation of the congregation, and taking part in more general public work. As I go on, it will be seen, that, so far from undervaluing these, I hold them to be all required even to produce a healthy pulpit power. Yet preaching is the central thing in our work. I believe in it, because Christ Himself set His stamp on it. Read His sayings, and you will see that this was what He sent forth the servants of His kingdom to do. "Christ," says St. Paul, "sent me not to baptize, but to preach the Gospel"; not, I think, thereby ignoring baptism, but putting it and all other ceremonies in their proper place of subordination to the preaching of the Word.

It is often charged against the evangelical, and especially the free, Churches, at the present day,

---

of their life. If ministers knew the silent appreciation of helpful preaching, they would work, if not harder, at least more brightly and hopefully. . . . Preachers should remember that the large silent part of their flock is only reached by preaching, and, therefore, they should give their strength to it, and not to little meetings. Suppose an average instance: Sunday morning attendance, 250. The minister does not preach well; but he works hard during the week, and has, Monday, Literary Society, 15; Tuesday, Young Ladies' Bible Class, 12; Wednesday, Prayer Meeting, 30; Thursday, Class for Servants, 8; Friday, Class for Children, 15. All told, these do not represent more than 50, leaving 200 reached only by preaching, and more or less dissatisfied."—*Ex sapientis manuscripto penes me.*

that they give preaching a position of too great prominence in public worship ; and we are counselled
to yield the central place to something else.   It is
put to us, for example, whether our people should
not be taught to come to church for the purpose of
speaking to God rather than in order to be spoken
to by a man.   This has a pious sound ; but there is
a fallacy in it.   Preaching is not merely the speaking
of a man.   If it is, then it is certainly not worth
coming to church for.   Preaching, if it is of the right
kind, is the voice of God.   This we venture to say
while well aware of its imperfections.   In the best
of preaching there is a large human element beset
with infirmity ; yet in all genuine preaching there is
conveyed a message from Heaven.   And, while it is
good for people to go to church that they may speak
to God, it is still better to go that He may speak to
them.   Nor, where God is authentically heard speaking to the heart, will the response of the heart in
the other elements of worship be lacking.   It is the
reception of God's message of free grace and redeeming love which inspires the true service of praise and
prayer ; and without this the service of the Church
is soulless ceremonial.*

* "New Testament preaching dates from the day of Pentecost.
Tongues of fire rested on the assembled Church ; and they began to
speak with other tongues, as the Spirit gave them utterance.   The word

From another side disparagement is frequently cast upon preaching in our day. It is said that the printing-press has superseded the preacher, and must more and more supersede him. Formerly, when people could not read, and literature was written only for scholars, the pulpit was a power, because it was the only purveyor of ideas to the multitude ; but now the common man has other resources : he has books, magazines, the newspaper : and he can dispense with the preacher. To this it might be answered, that the sermon is not the only thing which brings people to church. Where two or three are met together,

---

of God, the testimony of Jesus, the gospel of our salvation, preached in tongues of men of every race, was to be the form of power by which the kingdom of God, in our dispensation, should spread abroad and prevail. But the tongues were tongues of fire. This fire is, first of all, the Holy Spirit, whose quick, pure and living presence it denotes. But then it is intimated that the Holy Spirit was to prove Himself fire *in the speech of men.* It is intimated that human minds, as they uttered themselves to their fellows, and human speech in that utterance, were to prove capable of taking fire, so as to brighten and burn with the truth and power of God's Spirit. Such was the kind of preaching that was set a-going at Pentecost, and by it the world was to be won. Other forms of influence were not to be excluded, but this was to have the chief place. The word of power, coming burning-hot out of the living mouth of a believing man, is the leading form in which the Spirit's presence is evermore to make head in the Church against the world, and is to carry the Church on in her mission in the world. This gives us the fundamental view of our work as preachers ; and nothing more is needed in order to illustrate its dignity and glory."—PRINCIPAL RAINY.

there are influences generated of a spiritual and social
kind which answer to deep and permanent wants of
human nature. But there is an answer more direct
and conclusive. The multiplication of the products
of the printing-press and the possession by the
multitude of the power of reading them are certainly
among the most wonderful facts of modern times,
and, I will add without hesitation, among the most
gratifying. But what do they mean for the great
majority? In the days before the age of the press
arrived people only knew the gossip of their own
town, and this absorbed their thoughts and conversation. Now they hear every morning the gossip of
a thousand cities from China to Peru. The world
has become for the modern man immensely larger
and more interesting than it was to his predecessors;
and facts about it are accumulated on his mind in
overwhelming quantity and bewildering variety. But
does this make preaching less necessary to him? It
surely makes it far more necessary. He has more
need than his fathers had of those supersensible
principles which give order and meaning to sensible
facts. The larger and more wonderful the world
becomes, the more urgent becomes the question of
the cause which has produced it; and, the more the
figures multiply which the spectators have to watch
on the theatre of history, the more indispensable

becomes the knowledge of the argument of the drama. If the pulpit has an authentic message to deliver about Him whose thought is the ground of all existence, and whose will of love is the explanation of the pain and mystery of life, then, the more cultivated and eager the mind of man becomes, the more indispensable will the voice of the pulpit be felt to be ; and a real decay of the power of the pulpit can only be due either to preachers themselves, when, losing touch with the mysteries of revelation, they let themselves down to the level of vendors of passing opinion, or to such a shallowing of the general mind as will render it incapable of taking an earnest interest in the profounder problems of existence.

LECTURE II.

THE PREACHER AS A MAN OF GOD

LECTURE II.

THE PREACHER AS A MAN OF GOD

IN accordance with the plan announced yesterday, I am to turn your attention in the next four lectures to the prophets of the Old Testament as patterns for modern preachers; and the special subject for to-day is The Preacher as a Man of God.

To earnest minds at the stage at which you stand at present no question could be more interesting than this: How does a right ministry begin? what are the experiences which justify or compel a man to turn his back on all other careers and devote himself to this one? On the minds of some of you this question may be pressing at the present moment with great urgency. It is a question of supreme importance. In most things a good deal depends on beginning well; but nowhere is the commencement more momentous than here.

This is a point on which the greatest emphasis is laid in the history of the prophets. We are told how they became prophets. Their ministry commenced with a spiritual experience usually denominated the Prophetic Call.

Such experiences are narrated of the greatest prophets. The call of Moses was the scene of the Burning Bush, which is detailed at great length in his biography. The next outstanding prophet was Samuel, and there is no better known story in Scripture than the touching account of how the Lord called him to be the reformer of an evil age. Each of the three great literary prophets—Isaiah, Jeremiah and Ezekiel—has left an account of his own call; that of Ezekiel covering nearly three whole chapters. If the smaller prophets do not, as a rule, commemorate similar experiences of their own, it is not to be inferred that they did not pass through them. The brief compass of their writings is sufficient to account for the omission ; although perhaps a subjective element may also enter into the explanation. Among ourselves there are men who are able to confide to the public their own most sacred experiences, and habitually make use of them to illustrate and enforce the truth. To others nothing would be more unnatural : they shrink from the most distant allusion to the most sacred moments of their spiritual history. Yet these may be worth the whole world to themselves. Both modes of procedure have Scriptural warrant ; for some of the prophets narrate their calls, and others do not.

If these calls of distinguished men to God's service be noted one by one, they will be found to include many of the grandest scenes of Scripture. * There could be no more splendid subject—if I may give the hint in passing—for a course of lectures in the congregation, or even for a course, like the present, to students of divinity.

They exhibit astonishing variety. Moses, for example, was called in the maturity of his powers, but Samuel when he was still a child. Jeremiah's call bears a certain resemblance to that of Moses, because both resisted the Divine will through inability to speak ; but in other respects they are totally dissimilar. Ezekiel's stands altogether by itself, and is extremely difficult to unravel ; but it is thoroughly characteristic of his sublime and intricate genius. Nowhere else could there be found a more telling illustration of the diversity of operation in which the Spirit of God delights, when He is touching the spirit of man, even if He is aiming at identical results.

For in all cases the effect was the same. The man who was called to be a prophet was separated by

---

* " One great part of the history of the Bible is the history of Calls."— DEAN CHURCH.

this summons from all other occupations which could interfere with the service for which God had designated him. His whole being was taken possession of for the Divine purposes and subjected to the sway of the Divine inspiration. One of the commonest names of a prophet in the Old Testament is " a man of God." Through constant use this term has lost its meaning for us. But it meant exactly what it said : that the prophet was not his own, but God's man ; he belonged to God, who could send him wherever He wished and do with him whatever He would. It was the same idea that St. Paul expressed, when he called himself, as he loved to do, " the slave of Jesus Christ."

It has sometimes been attempted to explain these scenes away, as if they were not records of actual experience, but only poetic representations which the prophets prefixed to their writings, to afford their readers a dramatic prefiguration of the general scope of their prophecies, ideas being freely put into them which the prophets did not themselves possess at the commencement of their career, but only acquired by degrees as their life proceeded.* They are compared

---

* I am sorry to observe that even Mr. G. A. Smith, whose Commentary on Isaiah is distinguished not only by thorough scholarship but by what is far rarer in works of the kind—a profusion of just and inspiring ideas—at this point, following bad examples, says that there are ideas imported into the account of Isaiah's call which belonged to

to such efforts of the poets as the *Vision* of Robert
Burns, in which he tells how the muse of Caledonia
appeared to him at the plough and, casting her mantle
round him and claiming him as her own, consecrated
him the poet of his native land ; or the *Zueignung* of
Goethe, in which he feigns a similar experience which
befell him on the moonlight heights of the German
forest.   But, though there is a poetic element in
prophecy, the prophetic spirit was too much in earnest
for such figments of the imagination, which are alien
to the severity of the Hebrew genius.   Besides, such
scenes are not confined to the Hebrew prophets : they
belong to the true religion in all generations.

Any of the prophetic calls would bring suggestively
before us the topic with which we are occupied to-day ;
and it is not without regret that I turn away from the
Burning Bush, with its dramatic dialogue between
Jehovah and Moses touching many points which are
the very same as still perplex those who are standing
on the threshold of a ministerial career ; from the

---

a later period of his life. Not only is this wrong psychologically,
because it minimises the divinatory power of the human spirit in the
great moments of experience ; but surely it is utterly wrong artistically,
because, if the ideas are historically out of place, Isaiah himself ought
to have felt that, by placing them there, he was breaking the spell
of verisimilitude, on which the effect of such a picture depends.

chamber of the tabernacle, with its startling voice, in
which God opened the heart of Samuel to take in the
purpose of life ; and from the wonderfully instructive
scene in which the shrinking spirit of Jeremiah met
the Divine summons with the humble cry of depreca-
tion, "Behold, I cannot speak ; for I am a child," till
the Divine sympathy and wisdom answered his arguments and lifted him above his fears. But we have
agreed to take Isaiah as the representative of the
prophets ; and, in spite of these other attractions, we
need not repent of this ; for there is nothing in Holy
Writ more unique and sublime than the call of Isaiah,
and it is pregnant in every line with instruction. It
is, indeed, far away from us, and it will require a
strong effort to transport ourselves back over so many
centuries and enter sympathetically into the experience of one who lived in such a widely different world.
But it is a real chapter of human experience. As
Isaiah prophesied for fifty or perhaps even sixty years
after this, he must at the time have been in the prime
of his days. In short, he was at the very stage of
life at which you are now, and this is an account of
how a young man of three thousand years ago became
a public servant of God.

There are two or three points worth noting before
we go on to describe the scene itself.

1. It is reported in the sixth chapter of the prophecies of Isaiah. We should naturally have expected it to stand at the beginning of the whole book, as do the corresponding scenes in the books of Jeremiah and Ezekiel ; and it is not easy to say why it is not found in this position. We are perhaps too ready to think of the prophecies of a prophet as a continuous book, written, in one prolonged effort, on a single theme, as books are written in modern times. But this is a misconception. They came together more like the pieces of a lyric poet. A lyric poet composes his pieces at uncertain intervals of inspiration ; they range over a great variety of subjects ; and it may only be late in life that he thinks of collecting them in a volume. So the prophecies of the prophet came to him at uncertain and often lengthy intervals ; they were sometimes very brief, no longer than short lyrics ; and we know that he sometimes did not think of any literary publication of them till long after their oral delivery. A lyric poet, when collecting his pieces, may adopt anyone of several different principles of arrangement. The simplest way is to insert them in chronological order ; but he may follow some subtle psychological arrangement, as Wordsworth, for instance, did when his collected works were published ; or he may throw them together at random, according to the fancy of

the moment; and this is perhaps the commonest
case. There seems to be the same variety in the
prophets. The prophecies of Ezekiel, for example,
are arranged on the chronological principle, but
those of Isaiah and Jeremiah are not; and it is one
of the most difficult tasks of interpretation to assign
the different pieces to their original dates. It is
doubtful whether there is any rigid principle at all
in Isaiah's prophecies. It is even doubtful whether
the order in which they stand is due to him or
to a disciple or editor, who arranged them after he
was dead. We need hardly, therefore, inquire very
strictly why any particular chapter occurs in its
particular place. But it is somewhat awkward that
the sixth chapter stands where it does, in the body of
the book, instead of at the head of it; because this
hides its significance from the general reader. Scholars
are agreed, however, that it is an account of Isaiah's
call to be a prophet; and, when this is recognised,
every detail of the scene which it records is invested
with new meaning.

2. It is worthy of note that the event is precisely
dated. The chapter begins with the words, " In the
year that King Uzziah died." There are forms of
religious experience which are dateless—processes of
slow and unmarked growth, which may spread themselves over years; but there are also crises, when

experience crystallizes into events so remarkable that they become standing dates in the lives of those who have enjoyed them, from which they reckon, as other people do from birth or marriage or the turning-points of their domestic and commercial history.

Whether this was the first of such events in the history of Isaiah I have often wondered. There is nothing unlikely in the suggestion. In other cases the call to enter into God's work synchronized with the first real encounter with God Himself. Samuel's call to be a prophet coincided with his first personal introduction to acquaintance with Jehovah, whom, it is distinctly stated, he did not previously know ; and St. Paul's call to the apostolate happened at the same time as his conversion. As we go on, we shall come upon at least one circumstance which points pretty strongly to the conclusion that this was Isaiah's first conscious transaction with God.

3. The place where the incident occurred is also worthy of note. It was in the temple. Ewald and other able commentators interpret this to mean the heavenly temple, and suppose that the future prophet was transported to some imaginary place which he called by this name. But this is quite a gratuitous suggestion, and it very much weakens the impressiveness of the whole scene, the very point of which lies in the fact that it took place on familiar ground.

Isaiah was a Jerusalemite, and the temple was the
most familiar of all haunts to him. He had witnessed
there a thousand times the external ritual of religion
—the worshipping multitudes, the priests, and the
paraphernalia of sacrifice. But now, on the same
spot, he was to see a sight in whose glory all these
things would disappear. This is what the critical
moments of religious experience are always meant to
do : they obliterate the familiar externals of religion
and reveal the reality which is hidden behind them ;
they convert common spots of every-day experience
into the house of God and the gate of heaven.

Such were the circumstances of time and place in
which the crisis of Isaiah's history occurred. One
day, in the year that King Uzziah died, he wended
his way, as he had done hundreds of times before, to
the temple ; and there that took place which altered
the whole course of his life. Whether in the body or
out of the body, we cannot tell, he saw three successive visions, or rather a threefold vision—a vision of
God, a vision of sin, and a vision of grace.

1. It began with a Vision of God. The chapter
opens with these sublime words, " In the year that
King Uzziah died I saw the Lord." It is an astound-
ing statement to come from a prophet of that religion
whose fundamental principle was the spirituality of

God, "No man hath seen God at any time"; and, indeed, there is an old rabbinical tradition, that King Manasseh, who is said to have caused Isaiah to be sawn asunder, made the alleged impiety of these words the excuse for his cruelty. But it was a mere excuse; for the difficulty only serves to prove the transcendent spiritual tact and literary skill of the prophet, who manages the scene in such a way as to preserve quite intact the principle of the Divine spirituality. Though he says that he saw God, he gives no description of Him; only the sights and sounds round about Him are so described as in the most vivid way to suggest the Presence which remains unseen. It is as if a historical scene of ruin and conflagration were represented on canvas, without showing the burning materials, by painting the glare of light and the emotions of terror and dismay on the faces of the spectators.

First, the throne on which God sits is described: it is erected in the temple, and it is high and lifted up, for He is a great King. But no description is given of the Figure seated on it; only His train—the billowy folds of His robes—filled the temple. Above the throne, or rather round it, like the courtiers surrounding the throne of an Eastern monarch, stand the seraphim. These beings are mentioned only here in Holy Writ. Their name signifies the shining or fiery ones. They are attendants of the Divine King, bright and swift as fire in their intelligence and activity. Each has six wings : with twain he covers his face, and with twain he covers his feet, evidently to protect his eyes and person from the consuming glory of the Divine presence, which is thus indicated again without being described ; and with the remaining two he flies, or rather poises himself in his place ready for flight at the Divine signal.

Then, amidst these sublime sights break in sounds equally sublime. By our translation the impression is produced that they come from the seraphim. But the original is more vague, and the meaning probably is, that the responsive voices which are heard come from unseen choirs in opposite quarters of the temple. Unceasingly the strain rises from one side, unceasingly the answer comes from the other ; in the centre the voices meet and mingle in loud harmony.

Their burden is, " Holy, holy, holy, is the Lord of hosts ; the whole earth is full of His glory." That is, they are celebrating the two attributes of the Divine character which always most impressed a Jewish mind—His holiness and His omnipotence. The one is God as He is in Himself, turned inwards, so to speak. He is absolutely holy, unapproachable, a consuming fire scorching away impurity, falsehood, and sin of every kind. The other is God as He is in the world, turned outwards, so to speak ; the world's fulness—suns and systems, mountains and oceans, earthquake and storm, summer's abundance and winter's terror—all this is His glory, the garment by which He makes Himself visible.*

The voices swell till the temple rocks, or seems to rock to the reeling senses of the prophet, and the house is filled with smoke, or seems to be so, as a mist envelops the swooning spirit of the spectator. But still, through the mist, there peal, falling like the strokes of a hammer on the listening heart, the notes of the dread song, " Holy, holy, holy."

2. Next ensued a Vision of Sin. The vision of God could not but unseal a rushing stream of feeling of some kind in Isaiah. But of what kind would it be ? Surely of joyful adoration : the soul, inspired with the sublimity of these sights and thrilled with these sounds, will rise to the majesty of the occasion, and the human voice will strike in with all its force among the angelic voices, crying, " Holy, holy, holy."

So one might have expected. But the human mind is a strange thing ; and it is difficult to know where and how to touch its delicate and complex mechanism so as to produce any desired effect. You wish to

---

* This is the literal translation, " The fulness of the whole world is His glory."

produce a flow of tender feeling, and you tell a
pathetic tale, which ought, you think, to move the
heart.   But at every sentence the features of the
listeners harden into more and more rigidity, or even
relax into mocking laughter ; whereas the suggestion
of a noble thought, which seems to have nothing to
do with pathos, may instantaneously melt the soul
and unseal the fountain of tears.   Or is it the conscience which is to be affected ?   The clumsy operator
begins to assail it straight with denunciations of sin,
but, instead of producing penitence, he only rouses
the whole man into proud and angry self-defence ;
whereas a single touch, no heavier than an infant's
finger, applied away up somewhere, remote from
conscience, in the region of the imagination, may
send an electric shock down through the whole
being and shake the conscience from centre to
circumference.

Isaiah's mind was one of the most sensitive and
complicated ever bestowed on a human being ; but
it was now in the hands of its Maker, who knew how
to touch |it to fine issues.   The Maker's design on
this occasion was to produce in it an overpowering
sense of sin ; and what He did was to confront it with
infinite holiness and majesty.   These were brought so
near that there was no escape.   The poor, finite,
sinful man was held at arm's length, so to speak,

in the grasp of the Infinite and Most Holy ; and
the result was a total collapse of the human spirit.
Isaiah's eye turned away from the sight of God's
glory back upon himself, and back on his past life ;
and, in this light, all appeared foul and hideous.
There was sin everywhere—sin in himself and sin
in his environment. He was utterly confounded and
swallowed up of shame and terror. "Woe is me!"
he groaned, "for I am undone ; because I am a man
of unclean lips, and I dwell in the midst of a people
of unclean lips."

Why he felt the taint specially on his lips it might
not be easy to tell. Perhaps it was because the
angelic song was a challenge to join in the praise of
God, but he felt that the lips of one like him were
not worthy to join in their song. Perhaps—who
can tell ?—the besetting sin of his previous life may
have been profanity of speech, as it was evidently
a crying sin of his time. This suggestion gives a
shock to the ideas which we associate with Isaiah,
and it is hard to think that the lips which afterwards
spoke like angels can ever have defiled themselves
with such a sin. But this is the most natural meaning
of the words, and it is not against the analogy of
other lives. Great saints, and even great preachers,
are made out of great sinners ; and the memory of
an odious and conspicuous sin like this may some-

times lend a passionate force to subsequent devotion and keep alive for a lifetime the sense of personal unworthiness.

3. The last scene in the evolution of this vision, which was surely more than a vision, was the Vision of Grace. One of the fiery attendants, who hovered on quivering wing ready to execute the orders of the Divine King, receiving a command by some un-explained mode of communication, flew to the altar and, taking up the tongs, seized with them a stone from the altar fire. It was neither a coal, as our rendering gives it, nor a brand, but a heated stone, such as was used, and is used at the present day, in the East, for conveying heat to a distance for any purpose for which it might be required. It came from the altar : it contained God's fire, and God sent it.

The purpose for which it was required on this occasion was cleansing. Of cleansing there are in Scripture three symbols. The simplest is water ; and water can purify many things ; but there are some things which water cannot cleanse. A stronger agent is required, and this is found in fire. You must fling the ore, for example, into the fire, if you wish to extract from it the pure gold. There is a third symbol, which appears in the New Testament as well as the Old, and it is the most sacred of all.

It is blood. Water, fire, blood—these three mean the same in Scripture. In this case it was fire.

The seraph flew with the hot stone and laid it on the lips of the future prophet. Why did he lay it there? Because it was there that Isaiah felt his sin to be lying. He had said, "I am a man of unclean lips." The fire burned the sin away. So the seraph said, speaking in God's name, "Lo, this hath touched thy lips; and thine iniquity is taken away, and thy sin purged." It was the assurance of the Divine forgiveness, which had come swift as a seraph's flight in answer to Isaiah's confession.*

---

* The lips of Jeremiah were also touched in his call by the hand of God. But the meaning appears to have been different. He had complained that he could not speak—that he was tongue-tied. The touch of the Divine hand may have meant that the restraining cord was loosed, and a free passage made for the utterance of what he had to say. The words which accompanied the touch suggest, however, a slightly different idea—"Behold, I have put My words in thy mouth." The difficulty of Jeremiah was not exactly that of Moses, who, when he complained that he could not speak, meant that, never having acquired the art of expressing himself, he could not utter what he had to say, even though he was full of matter. This was the natural difficulty of an elderly man; for the art of expression has to be acquired in youth. But the difficulty of a young man like Jeremiah is not so much to express what he has to say as to get something worth saying. This was what Jeremiah complained of; and the touching of his lips meant that God was putting His own words into his mouth. It was a promise that the well of ideas in his mind should not run dry, but that God would give him such a revelation of His mind and will as would supply him with an ample message to his age. All three cases are full of instruction and encouragement.

Isaiah's preparation was completed in these three successive phases of experience ; and now the purpose was disclosed for which he had been prepared. From aloft—from the throne high and lifted up—came the question, " Whom shall I send, and who will go for us ? " The King needed a messenger to bear a message and represent Himself. He had chosen Isaiah to bear it ; yet He did not thrust the commission on him.* He did not need to do so ; for

---

* " After passing through the fundamental religious experiences of forgiveness and cleansing, which are in every case the indispensable premises of life with God, Isaiah was left to himself. No direct summons was addressed to him, no compulsion was laid on him ; but he heard the voice of God asking generally for messengers, and he, on his own responsibility, answered it for himself in particular. He heard from the Divine lips of the Divine need for messengers, and he was immediately full of the mind that he was the man for the mission, and of the heart to give himself to it. So great an example cannot be too closely studied by candidates for the ministry in our own day. Sacrifice is not the half-sleepy, half-reluctant submission to the force of circumstance or opinion, in which shape it is so often travestied among us, but the resolute self-surrender and willing resignation of a free and reasonable soul. There are many in our day who look for an irresistible compulsion into the ministry of the Church ; sensitive as they are to the material bias by which men roll off into other professions, they pray for something of a similar kind to prevail with them in this direction also. There are men who pass into the ministry by social pressure or the opinion of the circles they belong to, and there are men who adopt the profession simply because it is on the line of least resistance. From which false beginnings rise the spent force, the premature stoppages, the stagnancy, the aimlessness and heartlessness, which are the scandals of the professional ministry and the weakness of the Christian Church in our day. Men who drift into the

Isaiah had passed through a preparation which made him not only thoroughly able, but thoroughly willing. He had been lifted out of time into eternity ; and in this one hour of concentrated experience he had both died and been born again. His life had been undone and forfeited ; but God had given it back to him, and he felt that now it was not his own. He was thrilling with the power of forgiveness, and the impulses towards God—to be near Him, to serve Him, to do anything for Him—were now far stronger than his shrinking from Him had been a little before. Therefore of his own free will and choice he answered the Divine question with, " Here am I, send me."

Gentlemen, I have gone minutely into the details of this scene in the life of a representative preacher of the Old Testament, because every line of it speaks to the deep and subtle movements of our own experience. What is the inference to be drawn from it ? Is it that at the commencement of a preacher's career there must be a call to the ministry distinct

ministry, as it is certain so many do, become mere ecclesiastical flotsam and jetsam, incapable of giving carriage to any soul across the waters of this life, uncertain of their own arrival anywhere, and of all the waste of their generation, the most patent and disgraceful. God will have no driftwood for His sacrifices, no drift-men for His ministers. Self-consecration is the beginning of His service, and a sense of our own freedom and our own responsibility is an indispensable element in the act of self-consecration."—G. A. SMITH : *Isaiah.*

4

from the experience of personal salvation? This inference has often been drawn; but I prefer, in the meantime at least, to draw a wider, but, I believe, a sounder and more useful inference. It is this : that the outer must be preceded by the inner ; public life for God must be preceded by private life with God ; unless God has first spoken to a man, it is vain for a man to attempt to speak for God.

This principle has an extensive and varied application.

It applies to the beginnings of the religious life. I should like to be allowed to say to you, gentlemen, with all the earnestness of which I am capable, that the prime qualification of a minister is that he be himself a religious man—that, before he begins to make God known, he should first himself know God. How this comes to pass, this is not the place to explain. Only let me say, that it is more than the play upon us of religious influences from the outside. There must be a reaction on our own part—an opening of our nature to take in and assimilate what is brought to bear on us by others. There must be an uprising of our own will and a deliberate choice of God. Of course, in the history of many there are, at this stage, experiences almost as dramatic and memorable as this scene in the life of Isaiah ; and they may be composed of nearly identical elements.

In some haunt of ordinary life—perhaps in the church of one's childhood or in the room consecrated by the prayers of early years—there comes a sudden revelation of God, which transfigures everything. In this great light the man feels himself to be like an unclean thing, ready to be condemned and annihilated by the presence of the Thrice Holy. But then ensues the wonderful revelation of grace, when God takes up the soul in its despair and draws it to His heart, penetrating it with the sense of forgiveness and the confidence of childhood. It is not surprising that this new-born life should feel itself at once dedicated to the service of God. I heard one of our most rising ministers say a short time ago, that he knew he was to be a minister on the very day of his conversion, though at the time he was engaged in a totally different pursuit.

But this may come later ; and it may be the burden of another great moment of revelation. For, as I have hinted already in this lecture, the true Christian life is not all a silent, unmarked growth ; it has its crises also, when it rises at a bound to new levels, where new prospects unfold themselves before it and alter everything. There are moments in life more precious than days, and there are days which we would not exchange for years. Swept along with other materials into the common receptacle of memory, they shine like gold, silver, precious stones among the wood, hay, stubble of ordinary experience. It is impossible to say how much one such experience may do to direct and to inspire a life. I believe that many a humble minister has such an experience hidden in his memory, which he may never have disclosed to any one, but which is invested for himself with unfading splendour and authority, and binds him to the service of God till his dying day.*

But this principle, which we have drawn for our own use from Isaiah's call, applies not only to the initial act, but to every subsequent detail of our life. It is true of every appearance which a minister makes before a congregation. Unless he has spent the week with God and received Divine communica-

---

* I do not know that I have ever seen an entirely satisfactory statement of what constitutes a call to the ministry. Probably it is one of those things of the spirit which cannot be mathematically defined. The variety of the calls in Scripture warns us against laying down any scheme to which the experience of everyone must conform. It is the same as with the commencement of the spiritual life, where also the work of the Spirit of God overflows our definitions. While some can remember and describe the whole process through which they have passed, others who exhibit as undeniably the marks of the Divine handiwork can give comparatively little account of how it took place. The test of the reality of the change is not its power of being made into a good story. In the one case, however, as in the other, a conscientious man will give all diligence to make his calling and election sure. Excellent chapters on the subject will be found in Spurgeon's *Lectures to My Students* and Blaikie's *For the Work of the Ministry.*

tions, it would be better not to enter the pulpit or open his mouth on Sunday at all. There ought to be on the spirit, and even on the face of a minister, as he comes forth before men, a ray of the glory which was seen on the face of Moses when he came down among the people with God's message from the mount.

It applies, too, on a larger scale, to the ministerial life as a whole. Valuable as an initial call may be, it will not do to trade too long on such a memory. A ministry of growing power must be one of growing experience. The soul must be in touch with God and enjoy golden hours of fresh revelation. The truth must come to the minister as the satisfaction of his own needs and the answer to his own perplexities ; and he must be able to use the language of religion, not as the nearest equivalent he can find for that which he believes others to be passing through, but as the exact equivalent of that which he has passed through himself. There are many rules for praying in public, and a competent minister will not neglect them ; but there is one rule worth all the rest put together, and it is this : Be a man of prayer yourself ; and then the congregation will feel, as you open your lips to lead their devotions, that you are entering an accustomed presence and speaking to a well-known Friend. There are arts of study by which the contents of the Bible can be made available for the

edification of others ; but this is the best rule : Study
God's Word diligently for your own edification ; and
then, when it has become more to you than your
necessary food and sweeter than honey or the honey-
comb, it will be impossible for you to speak of it to
others without a glow passing into your words which
will betray the delight with which it has inspired
yourself.*

Perhaps of all causes of ministerial failure the
commonest lies here ; and of all ministerial qualifica-

---

* " You have to be busy men, with many distractions, wi.h time not
your own : and yet, if you are to be anything, there is one thing you
must secure. You must have time to enter into your own heart and be
quiet, you must learn to collect yourselves, to be alone with yourselves,
alone with your own though:s, alone with eternal realities which are
behind the rush and confusion of mortal things, alone with God. You
must learn to shut your door on all your energy, on all your interests,
on your hopes and fears and cares, and in the silence of your chamber
to ' possess your souls.' You must learn to look below the surface ; to
sow the seed which you wil never reap ; to hear loud voices against
you or seductive ones, and to find in your own heart the assurance and
the spell which makes them vain. Whatever you do, part not with the
inner sacred life of the soul whereby we live *within* to ' things not
seen,' to Christ, and truth and immortality. Your work, your activity,
belong to earth ; no real human interest, nothing that stirs or attracts
or that troubles men in this scene of life, ought to be too great or too
little for you. But your thoughts belong to heaven ; and it is to that
height that they must rise, it is *there* that in solitude and silence they
must be rekindled, and enlarged, and calmed, if even activity and
public spirit are not to degenerate into a fatal forgetfulness of the true
purpose of your calling—a forgetfulness of the infinite tenderness and
delicacy, of the unspeakable sacredness, of the mysterious issues, whi:h
belong to the ministry of souls."—DEAN CHURCH.

tions this, although the simplest, is the most trying. Either we have never had a spiritual experience deep and thorough enough to lay bare to us the mysteries of the soul ; or our experience is too old, and we have repeated it so often that it has become stale to ourselves ; or we have made reading a substitute for thinking ; or we have allowed the number and the pressure of the duties of our office to curtail our prayers and shut us out of our studies ; or we have learned the professional tone in which things ought to be said, and we can fall into it without present feeling. Power for work like ours is only to be acquired in secret ; it is only the man who has a large, varied and original life with God who can go on speaking about the things of God with fresh interest ; but a thousand things happen to interfere with such a prayerful and meditative life. It is not because our arguments for religion are not strong enough that we fail to convince, but because the argument is wanting which never fails to tell ; and this is religion itself. People everywhere can appreciate this, and nothing can supply the lack of it. The hearers may not know why their minister, with all his gifts, does not make a religious impression on them ; but it is because he is not himself a spiritual power.*

---

* "Habet autem ut obedienter audiatur quantacunque granditate dictionis majus pondus vita dicentis."—St. Augustine.

There comes to my mind a reminiscence from college days, which grows more significant to me the longer I live. One Saturday morning at our Missionary Society there came, at our invitation, to talk to us about our future life, the professor who was the idol of the students and reputed the most severely scientific of the whole staff. We used to think him keen, too, and cynical; and what we expected was perhaps a scathing exposure of the weaknesses of ministers, or a severe exhortation to study. It turned out, on the contrary, to be a strange piece, steeped in emotion and full of almost lyrical tenderness; and I can still remember the kind of awe which fell on us, as, from this reserved nature, we heard a conception of the ministry which had scarcely occurred to any of us before; for he said, that the great purpose for which a minister is settled in a parish is not to cultivate scholarship, or to visit the people during the week, or even to preach to them on Sunday, but it is to live among them as a good man, whose mere presence is a demonstration which cannot be gainsaid that there is a life possible on earth which is fed from no earthly source, and that the things spoken of in church on Sabbath are realities.

Side by side with this reminiscence there lives in my memory another, which also grows more beautiful the more I learn of life. It was my happiness, when

I was ordained, to be settled next neighbour to an aged and saintly minister. He was a man of competent scholarship, and had the reputation of having been in early life a powerful and popular preacher. But it was not to these gifts that he owed his unique influence. He moved through the town, with his white hair and somewhat staid and dignified demeanour, as a hallowing presence. His very passing in the street was a kind of benediction, and the people, as they looked after him, spoke of him to each other with affectionate veneration. Children were proud when he laid his hand on their heads, and they treasured the kindly words which he spoke to them. At funerals and other seasons of domestic solemnity his presence was sought by people of all denominations. We who laboured along with him in the ministry felt that his mere existence in the community was an irresistible demonstration of Christianity and a tower of strength to every good cause. Yet he had not gained this position of influence by brilliant talents or great achievements or the pushing of ambition ; for he was singularly modest, and would have been the last to credit himself with half the good he did. The whole mystery lay in this, that he had lived in the town for forty years a blameless life, and was known by everybody to be a godly and prayerful man. He was good enough to honour me with his friendship; and his example wrote deeply upon my mind these two convictions—that it may sometimes be of immense advantage to spend a whole lifetime in a single pastorate, and that the prime qualification for the ministry is goodness. *

* As he has been dead for several years, I need not hesitate to give the name of my dear and honoured friend—the Rev. James Black, of Dunnikier.

III.

THE PREACHER AS A PATRIOT

LECTURE III.

THE PREACHER AS A PATRIOT.

WE have committed ourselves, in our mode of dealing with the subject of these lectures, to the guidance of Scripture ; and I have already, in the opening lecture, alluded to the doubt, which might arise in some minds, that this method might carry us away from the living questions of the present age. But long experience has taught me to be very confident in this method of study. It is astonishing how directly, when trusting to the leading hand of Scripture, one is conducted to the heart of almost any subject, and how frequently one is thus compelled to take up delicate aspects of present questions which one would otherwise timidly avoid ; while there is, besides, this other great advantage, that one can always go forward with a firm step, having at one's back a Divine warrant and authority. To-day we shall have an illustration of this ; for the method which we are obeying will carry us straight into the midst of the burning questions of the hour; and the example of the prophets will press on our attention an aspect of ministerial duty which the times are urgently clamouring for, but which it is by no means easy to face. In the last lecture we were occupied with the call of the prophet to the service of God; to-day we have to study wherein consisted this service itself.

Here we are at once confronted with a contrast between the work of Old Testament prophets and that of modern ministers, to which it is by no means easy to adjust the mind. Our message in modern times is addressed to the individual; but the message of the prophets was addressed to the nation. The unit in our minds is always the soul; we warn every man to flee from the wrath to come; we reason and wrestle with him in the name of Heaven; we watch over the growth of his character; and we estimate our success by the number of individuals brought into the kingdom. In the prophets there is a complete absence of all this. They are no less in earnest; their aim is equally clear before them; but the unit in their minds is different: it is the Jewish state, or at least the city of Jerusalem, as a whole. A recent commentator* on Isaiah has raised the question, whether Isaiah has a gospel for the individual. He

---

* Rev. G. A. Smith.

makes out that he has; but it is in a somewhat round-about way; and it is not done without, to some extent, attributing to Isaiah a point of view which was not his. It was Christ who introduced the modern point of view. He was the discoverer of the individual. It was He who taught the world to believe in the dignity and destiny of the single soul; and He trained His ministers to seek and save it.

Isaiah's position, however, is well worth studying, and has its own lesson for us. Only we must acknowledge it to be what it really is, and endeavour to place ourselves on his standpoint. To him the New Testament position was no more possible than the modern view of ethics was to the ancient philosophers; and the student of philosophy, saturated from birth with the modern ideas of freedom and individuality, has an exactly similar difficulty to overcome, as he reads, for example, the *Republic* of Plato, where the state is everything and the individual nothing.

While a message to any individual is rare in the prophetical books, what we come upon wherever we open them is a patriotic and statesmanlike appeal on the condition of the country. The prophets addressed themselves by preference to the heads and representatives of the people, such as kings, princes and priests; because the power to effect changes in the situation of the country rested in their hands. But they also took advantage of large popular gatherings, and in some conspicuous place, such as the city-gate or the court of the temple, delivered their message, which thus might reach every corner of the land. A name which they delight to apply to themselves is Watchmen. As the watchman, stationed on his tower over the city-gate, kept guard over the safety of the place, giving notice when danger was approaching and summoning the citizens to defend themselves, so the prophets from their watch-tower—that is, the position of elevation and observation which inspiration gave them—watched over the weal of the state, observing narrowly its condition within, keeping their eye on the influences to which it was exposed from without, and, when danger threatened, giving the alarm. Their acquaintance is extraordinary with the state of every part of the country; and still more astonishing is their knowledge of surrounding countries. When they have to speak of Moab or Edom, they seem as familiar with the towns and rivers, the customs and history of these countries, as with those of Judah; and they appear to be as well acquainted with what is going on in the cities on the Nile or the Euphrates as with what is happening in Jerusalem. No home secretary is as well acquainted with the internal affairs of his own country, and no foreign secretary with the affairs of foreign countries.

It was their vocation to be sensitively alive to all the influences, near or remote, by which their native land could be affected.

The contents of the prophetic writings, notwith-standing their variety, easily fall into a few great masses. The chief are these three—Criticism, De-nunciation and Comfort.

1. There is a great mass of what may be called Criticism. Standing on their watch-tower and turn-ing their observation on the internal condition of the state, the prophets could nearly always discern dis-eased symptoms in the body corporate, and it was their duty to point them out. So Isaiah commences his prophecies : "The whole head is sick, and the whole heart faint. From the sole of the foot even unto the head there is no soundness in it ; but wounds, and bruises, and putrefying sores : they have not been closed, neither bound up, neither molli-fied with ointment." And he thus gives expression to the obligation which was laid on him to make these discoveries known : "Cry aloud, spare not, lift up thy voice like a trumpet, and show My people their transgression, and the house of Jacob their sins."

The sins which the prophets had to reprehend were pretty uniform all through the prophetic period ; and it is interesting to compare them with those

5

by which our own age is afflicted. There is no
school in which the conscience can be so well educated
to a sense of public sin as in the writings of the
prophets.

The root evil was always Idolatry. The nation
was continually falling away from the worship of the
true God to idols, or at least the worship of other
deities was incorporated with that of Jehovah. This
was always both a symptom of advanced degradation
and the head and fountain of other evils of the worst
kind. All the prophets attack it with all the weapons
in their armoury—with hot indignation and close
argument and scalding tears. Isaiah is remarkable
for attacking it with raillery and sarcasm. He takes
his readers into the idol workshop and details the
process of their manufacture. He shows us the
workmen, surrounded with their plates of metal and
logs of wood, out of which the god is to be fashioned,
and busy with their files and planes, their axes and
hammers, putting together the helpless thing. The
idolmaker, he says, has a fine ash or oak or cedar-
tree, and makes a pretty idol with it ; but with the
same wood he lights his fire and cooks his dinner—
" He burneth part thereof in the fire ; with part
thereof he eateth flesh ; he roasteth roast, and is
satisfied ; yea, he warmeth himself, and saith, Aha,
I am warm, I have seen the fire : and the residue

thereof he maketh a god, even his graven image : he falleth down unto it, and worshippeth it, and prayeth unto it, and saith, Deliver me ; for thou art my god."

Closely associated with idolatry was Luxury. So successful to our minds is the polemic of a prophet like Isaiah against idolatry that the wonder to us is that it was ever necessary ; and, indeed, there are few things more puzzling to the ordinary reader of Scripture than the constant lapses of the people of God into idolatry. How could they, knowing the true God, exchange a worship so rational and elevated for the worship of stocks and stones ? The explanation is a simple but a humiliating one. The worship of these foreign deities was accompanied with sensual excesses, which appealed to the strongest elementary passions of human nature. Feasts, dances and drunken orgies formed part of the worship of Baal and the other Canaanite divinities. Idolatry in Israel was never due to theoretic changes of opinion ; it was only the way in which an outbreak of laxity and luxury manifested itself. Its equivalent in our day would be an excessive development of the passion for amusement and excitement, destroying the dignity and seriousness of life. The wealthy and fashionable classes led the way, as they generally do in periods of moral retrogression ; and the worst symptom of all was when the womanhood of the country surrendered itself to the prevailing tendencies.   This last feature of degradation had developed itself in Isaiah's day ; and he attacks it with a strange combination of humour and moral indignation : " Because the daughters of Zion are haughty, and walk with stretched forth necks and wanton eyes, walking and mincing as they go, making a tinkling with their feet : therefore . . . the Lord will take away the bravery of their tinkling ornaments about their feet, and their cauls, and their round tires like the moon, the chains, and the bracelets, and the mufflers, the bonnets, and the ornaments of the legs, and the headbands, and the tablets and the earrings, the rings, and nose jewels, the changeable suits of apparel, and the mantles, and the wimples, and the crisping pins, the glasses, and the fine linen, and the hoods, and the veils.   And it shall come to pass, that instead of sweet smell there shall be stink ; and instead of a girdle a rent ; and instead of well set hair baldness ; and instead of a stomacher a girdle of sackcloth ; and burning instead of beauty."

Then there was Oppression.   Excessive luxury in the upper classes is usually accompanied with misery among those at the opposite end of the social scale ; because the rich in such a state of society are heartless, and not only neglect the poor, but oppress them. The prophets are full of the wrongs inflicted on the weak by the powerful. The wealthy landowners took advantage of the difficulties of their less prosperous neighbours to rob them of their holdings and remove the ancient landmarks ; and the courts of law were so corrupt that those who could not bribe the occupants of the chair of justice had no chance of redress. The spirit of the constitution was so far violated that the rich held their own fellow-countrymen in slavery, and did not even give them the advantage of the year of jubilee. Many a page of the writings of the prophets looks like a programme for the reform of abuses with which we are too familiar in our own civilisation. "Woe," says Jeremiah, "to him that buildeth his house by unrighteousness, and his chambers by wrong ; that useth his neighbour's services without wages, and giveth him not for his work."

Last of all there was Hypocrisy. In spite of these sins, crying to Heaven, there was seldom any lack of religiosity or the outward forms of religion. Religion was divorced from morality, and ritual was substituted for righteousness. There is no commoner or weightier burden in the prophets than this. It is on this subject that Isaiah lets loose the whole force of his prophetic soul in his very first chapter, where there is a truly appalling picture of the combination of religious rites the most multiplied with moral abuses the most clamant : " To what purpose is the multitude of your sacrifices unto Me ? saith the Lord : I am full of the burnt-offerings of rams, and the fat of fed beasts ; and I delight not in the blood of bullocks, or of rams, or of he-goats. When ye come to appear before Me, who hath required this at your hand, to tread My courts? Bring no more vain oblations ; incense is an abomination unto Me ; the new moons and sabbaths, the calling of assemblies, I cannot away with ; it is iniquity, even the solemn meeting. Your new moons and your appointed feasts My soul hateth : they are a trouble unto Me ; I am weary to bear them. And when ye spread forth your hands, I will hide Mine eyes from you : yea, when ye make many prayers, I will not hear : Your hands are full of blood. Wash you, make you clean ; put away the evil of your doings from before Mine eyes ; cease to do evil, learn to do well ; seek judgment, relieve the oppressed, judge the fatherless, plead for the widow."

Thus did these watchmen search out the moral and religious condition of the people to the very bottom and, in the most expressive language, bring home to their fellow-countrymen how they stood in the eyes of God.

2. A second large mass of the prophetic writings is occupied with Denunciation, or the prediction of

calamities about to come as the punishment of sin. As sure as the prophets were that the God of the universe was a righteous God, so certain were they that the public sins which they exposed would bring down the wrath of Heaven ; for " though hand join in hand, the wicked shall not be unpunished."

The instruments of punishment were not far to seek. Israel was surrounded by nations which entertained towards her feelings of bitter hostility and needed only the slightest provocation to attack her. Such were Edom and Moab, Philistia and Syria. But, above all, she was hemmed in on both sides by great and warlike powers—Egypt on the one hand and Assyria or Babylonia on the other. These were incessantly watching each other, and, in doing so, they had to look across Israel. She lay in the way which the one had to take in order to get at the other. The secular historian would say that she could not but fall sooner or later into the hands of the one or the other, and that she would probably pass frequently from hand to hand. But to the prophets these warlike powers were the scourges in God's hand to punish the sins of His people ; and, looking outwards from their watch-tower, after exposing the sins within the state, they announced that the storm-cloud of calamity was rising from this quarter or that long before any suspicion of it had dawned

on the citizens themselves.   Jehovah turns the hearts
of kings and peoples as the rivers of water, and He
stirred up these hostile nations when His people
were in need of chastisement ; He could wield their
power as the axe which assails a tree is wielded by
the woodman ; He could call the mightiest conqueror
to serve His secret purposes, as a man calls a dog to
his foot.*   They did not know that they were being
thus used.   They had their own designs, and their
hatred and cruelty towards God's people were real
enough.   They were even, after doing God's work on
His people, to be punished in turn for the animosity
and violence with which they performed it.   But in
the meantime the will of Jehovah was accomplished,
and the discipline of His providence wreaked on the
sins of the nation.

3. The third great element in these books is
Comfort.   Not unfrequently, in delivering these pre-
dictions of approaching calamity, the prophets had
to put themselves into opposition to popular forms
of patriotism and incur the danger of being regarded
as enemies of their country.   This was especially the
case with Jeremiah, who was burdened all his life
with the sad task of proclaiming that the time for
repentance was past, and that the Jewish state, with

* These are Isaiah's images,

its capital, must be destroyed. When the enemy was before the walls of Jerusalem, and the heads of the state were rallying the citizens to the last and most sacred duty of defending their hearths and altars, he had still to predict that resistance was useless ; and he was imprisoned as a traitor, because his words were disheartening the soldiers. When at last the city fell into the hands of the enemy, he was set free from imprisonment and loaded with honours by the conqueror as one who had been a valuable ally. Never was a position more equivocal occupied by a patriot. Yet never has there beaten in a human breast a heart more patriotic than Jeremiah's. Patriotism, strong as a man's passion and tender as a woman's love, is the keynote of every chapter of his prophecies. This is characteristic of all the prophets. They loved Israel, and especially the city of Jerusalem, with an ardour of affection such as has rarely, if ever, been bestowed on any other country or city on earth. There was something natural in this passion ; for Palestine was a lovely country, whose fruitful plains and picturesque valleys and vine-clad hills easily captivated the hearts of its inhabitants ; and Jerusalem was a city beautiful for situation. But this natural attachment was transfigured into a higher sentiment. Jerusalem was the hearth and sanctuary of the true religion. The country was dear to the hearts of the prophets, because it had been specially chosen by Jehovah as a home for His people, in which they might work out their destiny. The people who inhabited this country were to be married to Jehovah; He was to penetrate them with His spirit and character; and in them and their seed all nations of the earth were to be blessed.

To this sublime conception of the nation the hearts of all the prophets clung. However unworthy of it their own generation might be, they believed in the inexhaustible resources of their race, which was immortal till its destiny was accomplished. It was this faith, inspiring Isaiah, which enabled him to rally his fellow-countrymen to the defence of Jerusalem, when, according to all human probabilities, extinction stared it in the face. And even Jeremiah, though he had to predict the ruin of the city of his heart, never dreamed for a moment that its career was at an end; but, looking beyond the calamities of the immediate future, he predicted that God would restore the captivity of His people and yet make Zion a praise in the earth. It was, indeed, in times of calamity and suffering that the patriotism of the prophets burned most ardently. It was then that, speaking in God's name, they poured out on the stricken city the affection which breathes in such wonderful words of Isaiah as these : " Can a mother forget her sucking child, that she should not have compassion on the son of her womb? Yea, they may forget; yet will I not forget thee. Behold, I have graven thee upon the palms of My hands; thy walls are continually before Me." The second half of Isaiah,* addressed to the exiles in Babylon, overflows with such outbursts of tenderness ; and, although there is obviously a love in them which is more than human, yet the Divine love could not have found an outlet and a voice for itself except through a human heart of the most exquisite sensibility and passionate patriotism.† The prophets, who could scourge the people in the height of their prosperity and wantonness with words which smote like swords, became in the days of calamity the assiduous ministers of comfort, pouring balm into the wounds of their country and never allowing the daughter of Zion to despair of her future.

It was then especially that they cultivated the most remarkable of all the elements of prophecy—the hope

---

* For our purpose in these lectures it is of no consequence whether there were two Isaiahs or only one. We are seeking to ascertain the leading features of the prophets ; and, if we attribute to one person qualities which were distributed among two, this will matter little, as long as they are typical qualities of the prophet.

† " The tale of the Divine Pity was never yet believed from lips that were not felt to be moved by human pity."—GEORGE ELIOT.

of the Messiah. Tragic as was the failure of the
prophets themselves to raise the nation to the elevation which they saw so clearly to be her destiny, they
all believed that what they had failed to do would
yet be done, and that there would yet be a Jerusalem
bright and glorious as a star, and serving as the star
of hope to all the peoples of the earth. Their confidence in this did not rest solely on the will and
power of God in general; it was guaranteed to them
by the belief, which, under different forms, they all
cherished, and taught their countrymen to cherish,
that in the womb of the nation there lay One, to be
born in due time, endowed with powers far greater
than their own, who would take up the task which
each of them had had in his turn to lay by unaccom-
plished, and carry it forward to its fulfilment—a Child
of the nation who would unite in His character all
the attributes in their fullest perfection which the
nation herself ought to have possessed, and who,
though standing high above His fellow-countrymen,
would yet be thoroughly incorporated with them, and,
taking on His shoulders the responsibility of their
destiny, would never fail or be discouraged under it,
but bear it victoriously to the goal. "Unto us a
Child is born, unto us a Son is given; and the
government shall be upon His shoulders; and His
name shall be called Wonderful, Counsellor, the

Mighty God, the Everlasting Father, the Prince of Peace."

Now, gentlemen, the question is, How far the aspect of the prophetic activity which we have considered to-day is a model to us?

It might be argued that this is a stage of preaching which has been superseded, and that the message of ministers ought now to be addressed entirely to individuals. This is the theory of preaching on which many act, without perhaps considering how widely it differs from the procedure of the prophets. And no doubt much might be said in its defence. It was a vast step in the development of religion when Jesus turned from the nation to the individual and taught the world the value of the soul. The stress of Christian preaching must ever lie here; the preacher is not worthy of the Christian name who does not know what it is to hunger and thirst for the salvation of individuals, and who does not esteem the salvation of even one soul well worth the labour of a lifetime.

Still it may be doubted whether any stage through which preaching has passed can ever be entirely superseded; and we may well hesitate to believe that the work of an Isaiah or a Jeremiah is not still work for us.

This doubt is further strengthened when we turn to the record of Christ's own preaching. He is the final standard and incomparable model. But, though He discovered the soul and taught the world the value of the individual, His preaching was not exclusively directed to individuals. It had a public and national side. He cast His protection over publicans and sinners, not only because they were the children of men, but also because they were the seed of Abraham; He submitted His claims to the ecclesiastical authorities of the nation, and, when they rejected them, He directed against the religious parties the thunderbolts of His invective. The tears and words of indescribable tenderness which He poured out upon the city where He was about to be martyred proved that the patriotism of Isaiah and Jeremiah still burned in His heart; and He charged His apostles, when sending them forth to evangelize the world, to begin at Jerusalem.*

If this did not settle the question, the nature of the case would demonstrate that the preacher's vocation includes a message to the community as well as to

* Not to mention the social element in His preaching comprehended in the doctrine of the Kingdom of God. The comparative absence of the patriotic element from apostolic preaching is chiefly due to the fact that the apostles were missionaries in cities and countries where they were strangers. In some respects modern ministers in settled charges are liker the prophets than the apostles.

the individual. It will be conceded by all that the preacher exists for the promotion of righteousness and the diminution of sin in the world. But sin is not only lodged in the heart of the individual ; it is embodied also in evil customs and unjust laws, for which the community is responsible. The individual is largely moulded by his environment ; but this may either be so favourable to goodness that his evil tendencies are restrained and everything encourages him to do well, or so evil that the worst vices are easily contracted, while every step in the right direction meets with a storm of opposition. No one would contend that the chances of a soul are the same whether it lives among those who watch carefully over its development and guide its footsteps in the paths of peace, or among those whose word and example are encouragements to every kind of sin. Society ought to be a kindly matrix in which incipient life is nurtured into health and beauty ; but it may be a malignant nurse, by whom the stream of life is poisoned at its very source. If this be so, then it is as reprehensible in those whose vocation is to watch over the moral and spiritual development of their fellow-men to be indifferent to the conditions by which life is surrounded as it would be discreditable to the physicians of a city swept year after year by pestilence, if they took no interest in the insanitary conditions to which the epidemic was due, but lazily contented themselves with curing their own patients.

We seem to have arrived at precisely the point in the Church's history when her mind and conscience are to awake to this aspect of her duty. One of the most eminent members of the English bench of bishops said recently, that the social question is the question which the Christianity of the present day has to solve ; and this sentiment is being echoed in every quarter. Strange it is how age after age one word of the message of Christianity after another lays hold of the Christian mind and becomes for a time the watchword of progress. There can be little doubt that this is the word for our age. The extraordinary response given throughout the civilised world to General Booth's *In Darkest England* proves how deeply the conscience of the world is being stirred by the misery and degradation of the outcasts of society.

General Booth's book, and other books and pamphlets like it, have brought home to us the fact, that at the base of our civilisation there is sweltering a mass of sin and misery, which is not less a reproach to Christianity than were the publicans and sinners to the religion of the contemporaries of Christ; because, though the Church may not, like the Scribes and Pharisees, despise and hate these outcasts, it has not yet coped effectually with the problem of their condition ; and perhaps their numbers are increasing rather than diminishing. There are sections of the community in which the conditions of existence are so evil that childhood is plunged, almost as soon as it is born, into an element of vice and crime, the bloom of modesty is rudely rubbed off the soul of womanhood, and manhood is so beset with temptation that escape is well-nigh impossible. Can anyone doubt that an Isaiah or a Jeremiah would, in such a state of society, have lifted up his voice like a trumpet and cast the condition of these lost children of our people in the face of the luxurious rich, and especially of the professors of religion ? And is it less obvious that this is still the duty of the modern pulpit ?

It cannot, indeed, be said with truth, that the Church has not faced the problem. There is one of the causes of social misery, and that the very chief, against which the Church, especially in your country, has nobly asserted herself. Drink is the cause to which magistrates and judges, and all who are brought directly into contact with the fallen and criminal classes, attribute three-fourths of the evils of society. Drink is the despair of every Christian worker who has ventured down among the pariahs of our civilisation. Against this the Churches have not been inactive. But we are just beginning to acknowledge that, though drunkenness is the great cause of

6

misery, there are other causes behind it which must
likewise be coped with. Why do the people drink?
This question, when it is impartially considered, will
bring many abuses of our social system into view,
which must be put out of the way before the evils of
drunkenness can be stopped. Excessively prolonged
labour exhausts the system and makes it crave for
artificial stimulus. Excessively low wages, with no
prospect of rising in the world, beget a spirit of reck-
lessness, which makes men ready to turn to anything
that promises to bring a gleam of sunshine into
their monotonous lot. Ill-furnished and insanitary
abodes drive forth their inmates to seek the bright-
ness and comfort of the saloon. These are specimens
of the new questions which demand the attention of
those who feel the reproach of our defective civilisation.

There is one type of remedy which the Church has
liberally supplied. To those already fallen she has
extended a helping hand. The Evangelical Revival
produced a spirit of philanthropy which has invented
schemes for the relief of every form of human woe ;
and these have multiplied to almost unmanageable
numbers. But we are beginning to see that, multiply
them as we may, they must be totally insufficient as
long as the causes of misery are undealt with. If
the causes remain as strong as ever, new victims

will be manufactured as fast as philanthropy can rescue those already made. The time has come to ascend higher up the stream than has hitherto been done, and cut it off at its source. In other words, we must direct the whole force of Christian philanthropy to the stopping of the causes of social misery.

For this work new weapons will be required ; and perhaps the principal of these will· be legislation. The prophets appealed, as I have said, to kings and princes, because in their hands lay at that time the force of government. But this power has now passed, and is daily more completely passing, into the hands of the people, on whom lies the responsibility which formerly lay elsewhere. And, if we are to follow in the footsteps of Isaiah and Jeremiah, ·we must teach the people to rise to their responsibility and make use of the weapon which time has put into their hands for altering the conditions of life. They must send to the seats of authority, both in the municipality and in the state, men of a public spirit, who will act not for their own interest or for the interest of faction, but for the good of the whole community ; and they must see to it, that the laws and their administration are such as will make evil-doing difficult and well-doing easy.

Of course this will involve conflict ·with those

interests which are vested in abuses ; for there are trades which flourish on the poverty of the poor and even the vices of the vicious. These enjoy, in many cases, the advantage of high social standing; and many of the organs of public opinion will rally to their support. But the Church must appeal to the Christian conscience and summon forth the resources of Christian virtue, to meet this new phase of the task which has been appointed her. Christianity has always, and especially during the last hundred years, had the open hand of charity ; but she will need, during the next hundred years, to have also a hand which can close itself firmly over the instrument of government, and make use of it as a lever for lifting out of the way many great obstacles which are keeping back the Kingdom of God.

I am quite aware of the dangers of this new departure which I am advocating. There is the great danger of undervaluing the work of saving individual souls. There is the danger of forsaking the Word of God and converting the pulpit into an organ of secular discussion ; although, on the other hand, there are numerous portions of the Bible which directly raise the discussion of social problems and, when otherwise applied, can only be interpreted in a more or less unnatural sense. There is the danger of making the minister the mouthpiece of a party. Christian tact and discretion will be necessary at every step. But surely this is no reason for declining our duty, but only a reason for bringing out all our resources.

One consideration which simplifies the problem is, that it is not so much the place of the minister to intervene in special questions as to beget in his people a public and patriotic spirit, and to teach them to look upon the discharge of the duties of citizenship as a part of Christianity. When our people have been brought to recognise that the public weal is their concern, and that they are responsible for the state of society and the conditions of life, they can be left to themselves to choose the right men and support the right measures.*

Here we can build on a natural foundation. It is natural for a man to be attached to the place of his birth or the town in which he lives. The roots of his life are in its soil; his interests bind him to it; and,

---

* For example, there will rarely be any delicacy at the time of an election in urging on the people that it is their duty to go to the poll, but it will nearly always be an unpardonable indiscretion to indicate from the pulpit for whom they should vote. Very often good causes are lost, or long delayed, not because the sentiment of the electorate is opposed to them, but because large numbers are too apathetic to vote at all.

if he be at all divinely-souled, its traditions and notable names cannot fail to lay hold upon his heart. The chances which a city has of getting its affairs well attended to are measured by the number of its inhabitants who are animated with such sentiments. In the same way, it is natural for a man to love his country. Some countries especially have the power of casting such a spell over the hearts of their children as binds them to their service. Of my country this might be said. Small as it is, its beauty, its history and its romantic associations wield over the hearts of its inhabitants an extraordinary attraction. Perhaps part of the secret may lie in its very smallness ; for feeling contracts a passionate force within narrow limits, as our Highland rivers become torrents within their rocky beds. Of your country also it might be said for different reasons. America stirs patriotic sentiment, not by its smallness, but by its largeness and wonderful variety ; not by the memories of the past, but by the boundless possibilities of the future.

These sentiments exist in the minds of our people already ; and we only need to foster them and impregnate them with a Christian element, in order to produce convictions about public duty which would have the most blessed results. We might train our people to feel keenly the woe of mankind and especially

the moral blots on the fair fame of their own city
or country.   We might get them to cherish a high
ideal of what the place of their abode should be,
morally and spiritually, and of what their country
might do in the world.   In Scotland there was such
an ideal once : the eye of the dying Covenanter saw,
painted on the mist of the moorland, the vision of
a consecrated land ruled by a covenanted king.*   In
England it existed once, in the Puritan days, when,
as Richard Baxter says, England was like to become
a land of saints, a pattern of holiness to the world,
and the unmatchable paradise of the earth.   You had
it in America once : when your fathers landed in the

---

* "When I would cast my mind back to what we have earned and
reaped from these men, it strikes me perhaps more than anything
which I have yet named, that we should thank them for the passionate
quest of a glorious ideal.   It is such ideals, even when they are un-
attainable, which lift up the character of men and nations.   I think
that no worthy historian has yet been found to tell, as it ought to be
told, how much Scotland owes to this splendid vision which these men
sought, the vision of a consecrated land of saints ruled by a covenanted
king, loyal to Christ.   It hovered before the rapt eyes of these saints
of Scotland until it well-nigh turned them into seers, it elevated them
until it made them heroes, and though the picture seemed to fade
before the eyes of their children, as though it had been painted by the
morning light on the mist of their own moorland, still, it has done
its work, for it has contributed mightily to educate the hearts of
Scotchmen.   But has it so faded ?   Or is it not simply thrown forward,
as the old Jew learned to throw his Messianic hopes forward, from one
anticipated Christ to another, better and greater, yet to come ? "—
J. Oswald Dykes, D.D.

Mayflower, they were seeking not merely meat and drink, or even wealth and plenty, but a home in which their descendants might grow up in freedom, virtue and religion. We must get that ideal back again, if, in spite of railroads and industrial armies and wealth beyond the dreams of avarice, we are not to become corrupt and ready to be swept away with the besom of destruction. We might train every man on whom our message lays hold to live with the conviction that it is his duty, before he dies, to do something to make his own town more beautiful, his country happier, and the world better.

As I am addressing some who may before long be wielding a great influence, let me add one suggestion. In matters such as I have been speaking of to-day success comes to the man who has a programme. Now is the time, when you are looking out on the world with the keen eyes of youth, to note the abuses which need correction and to picture with the eye of the imagination the improvements which are required to wipe out the reproach or to elevate the reputation of your country. Fix the vision in the centre of your mind ; keep it ever before you ; and your dream may change to a reality which will modify the conditions of life for whole generations of your fellow-men. What could be worthier of your manhood at its present stage than to be revolving some plan for the benefit and honour of your country? Even if it should never come to anything, it will be good that it has been in your heart. But there is nothing else which is more likely to come to something. "What," says Alfred de Vigny, "is a great life? It is a thought conceived in the fervent mind of youth and executed with the solid force of manhood."

IV.

THE PREACHER AS A MAN OF THE WORD

LECTURE IV.

THE PREACHER AS A MAN OF THE WORD.

GENTLEMEN, in the lecture before last I spoke of the prophet's call to the service of God, and in last lecture of the work itself which he had to do. To-day I am to speak of the instrument with which he did it.

This was the Word; the prophet was a Man of the Word. In accomplishing his great and difficult work he wielded no other weapon. It seems the frailest of all weapons; for what is a word? It is only a puff of air, a vibration trembling in the atmosphere for a moment and then disappearing. But so might one speak of the cloud whose rolling coils of vapour, changing every moment, seem the least substantial of all things; yet out of it breaks the forked lightning, which rives the giant of the forest, and overturns the tower which has defied ten thousand assailants, and, loosening the crag, sends it thundering down the mountain-side. Though it be only a weapon of air, the word is stronger than the sword of the warrior.

Words have overturned dynasties and revolutionised kingdoms. When the right virtue is in them, they outlast every other work of man. Where are the cities which were flourishing when David sang? where are the empires whose armies were making the world tremble when Isaiah wrote? Nineveh and Babylon, Tyre and Memphis—where are they? But the Psalms of David still delight, and the wisdom of Isaiah still instructs, the world.

The prophets were well aware of the temper and force of this weapon which they wielded. Jeremiah refers with especial frequency to the power of the word. " Is not My word," he asks, " like as a fire, saith the Lord ; and like a hammer that breaketh the rock in pieces?" When putting this weapon into his hand, the Lord said to him, " See, I have set thee over the nations and over the kingdoms, to root out, and to pull down, and to destroy, and to throw down, to build, and to plant." How was one man to be able to throw down and build up kingdoms? He speaks as if he were at the head of irresistible legions and equipped with all the enginery of war. But so he was ; for all these and more are in the word. Such military notions seem to have occurred naturally to the wielders of it. Another of them says, " The weapons of our warfare are not carnal, but mighty through God to the pulling down of strongholds ;

casting down imaginations, and every high thing that exalteth itself against the knowledge of God, and bringing into captivity every thought to the obedience of Christ." Yet another of them says, " The word of God is quick and powerful, and sharper than any two-edged sword." And Isaiah says, in the name of the Servant of the Lord, " He hath made my mouth like a sharp sword ; in the shadow of His hand hath He hid me, and made me a polished shaft ; in His quiver hath He hid me." *

The word of the prophets has two aspects : it is, on the one side, a Message from God, and, on the other, a Message to Men.

1. The word which the prophets wielded was the word of God. Herein lay the secret of its power. For the word of God is the thought of God ; and this is more ancient than the stars and lies more deeply embedded in the constitution of things than the roots of the mountains ; it is the prop by which the universe is sustained. God's word is before all things, for it created them ; and His thoughts are the rails on which the course of the world runs.

It was the privilege of the prophets to approach so

---

* The Servant of the Lord is a prophet ; and in the descriptions of him in this character we can perhaps best see what was Isaiah's conception of a prophet. See especially ch. lxi. 1-3.

near to God, to enter so completely into sympathy and fellowship with Him, and to know so clearly what were His purposes, that their own thoughts became identical with His; and, therefore, when they spoke, their words were God's words. Not only do they preface many of their utterances with "Thus saith the Lord," but—what is far more strange—they often begin, without any preface, and go on speaking in the first person singular, when not the prophet but Jehovah is the speaker; as if their personality were so enveloped in His as to disappear altogether.[*]

But this remarkable knowledge of the thoughts of God was not given to the prophets for themselves. The philosopher may shut himself up in secret to study the laws of the universe and keep his conclusions to himself; and even the poet perhaps may be so happy in his own vision of beauty that he does not care to utter his song to the world; but not so the prophet. He, indeed, was also, in the strictest sense, an original thinker, and the new conceptions of God which he was privileged to convey to the world dawned upon his own mind with that secret delight which makes the creative thinker feel himself to be

> Like some watcher of the skies
> When a new planet swims into his ken.

One of the prophets gives expression to this secret

---

[*] See Ewald's Introduction to *The Prophets*.

joy when he says, " Thy words were found, and I did eat them ; and Thy words were unto me the joy and the rejoicing of mine heart " ; and, after a night spent in receiving revelations, he says, " On this I awaked and beheld, and my sleep was sweet unto me." But the knowledge of God's mind and will which the prophets obtained was not for themselves, but for others. It was not abstract knowledge, but a knowledge of God's will about the course of history—about " what Israel ought to do." It was, in short, not only a revelation, but a message.

Hence, one of the most outstanding characteristics of the prophets was the sense of being ambassadors charged with a communication which they were bound to deliver. If those to whom they were sent with it welcomed them, good and well ; but, if not, they were not absolved from their duty. The man who speaks to men for his own ends—to obtain influence in the management of their affairs or to display his talents and win a name —will go on speaking as long as they are inclined to listen ; but, if they do not appreciate his efforts, or if he wearies of the employment, he can betake himself to retirement and be heard no more. But a prophet could not act thus. His message might arouse bitter opposition, and often did so : " Woe is me, my mother," exclaims Jeremiah, " that thou hast borne

7

me a man of strife and a man of contention to the whole earth." Gladly would he have withdrawn from the contest, if he could, and sought a lodge in some vast wilderness. But the sense of being a messenger drove him on: "Then I said, I will not make mention of Him, nor speak any more in His name; but His word was in mine heart as a burning fire shut up in my bones; and I was weary with forbearing, and I could not stay."

This was what lent the prophets the wonderful courage which characterized them. They forgot themselves in their message. The fire of God in their bones would not permit them to hesitate. Whether it was a frowning king or an infuriated mob the prophet had to brave, he set his face like a flint. Comfort, reputation, life itself might be at stake; but he had to speak out all that God had told him, whether men might hear or whether they might forbear.

2. The other aspect of the prophets' word was that it was a Message to Men. If, on the one hand, the word of the prophets was a power because it was the word or thought of God, it depended, on the other hand, for its effect on becoming a word which those to whom it was communicated could repeat in their own vocabulary and thereby turn into a thought of their own; for it was only when men's minds were

so modified by the prophets' words that they began, in their degree, to think the thoughts of God, that the prophetic message became an influence in their life. The prophet had, therefore, to stand in a double attitude, and a double process had to be performed in his mind. He had, in the first place, to turn himself wholly round to God and away from the world, and clear his mind of everything else, that he might receive the message in its purity ; but then he had, in the second place, to turn himself round towards men and, taking their circumstances into account, deliver the message to them in the most effective way. He had first to allow the Divine message to master him ; but then he had to turn upon it and master it, before he could be the medium by which it was conveyed to others.

The prophets had to go amongst men, even if it were at the risk of life, and deliver the Divine message. They had to use every device to make it telling, striking in at every opportunity and giving line upon line, precept upon precept, here a little and there a little. They did not disdain the homeliest means, if it served the purpose. A prophet would go about in public carrying a yoke on his neck, like a beast of burden, or lie a whole year on his side, to attract attention to some important truth. More than once we find a prophet setting up a board in the market-

place, with only a few words written on it, into which
he had condensed his message, that the passers-by
might read it.

On the other hand, when it was appropriate, they
did not spare themselves the trouble of cultivating
the graces of style by which words are made attractive
and impressive.* The prophetic books are almost
as artistic as poems. Their literary form is not
exactly poetry, though now and then it crosses its
own boundary and becomes poetical. It is a kind of
rhythmical prose, governed by laws of its own, which
it carefully observes. All the prophets are not, indeed,
equally careful. Some of them appear to have been
too completely carried away with the message which
they had to deliver to think much of the way of
delivering it. But these were not the strongest of
the prophets ; and it is worth observing, that those
who took the most pains about the form in which
what they had to say was couched have been the
most successful prophets in this sense, that they have
been most read by subsequent generations.

---

* "Bonorum ingeniorum insignis est indoles, in verbis verum
amare, non verba. Quid enim prodest clavis aurea, si aperire quod
volumus non potest ? Aut quid obest lignea, si hoc potest, quando
nihil quærimus, nisi patere quod clausum est ? Sed quoniam inter
se habent nonnullam similitudinem vescentes atque discentes, propter
fastidia plurimorum etiam ipsa sine quibus vivi non potest alimenta
condienda sunt."—St. Augustine.

At the head of them all, in this respect, stands Isaiah. If the book of an ordinary reader of the Bible were examined, it would be found, I imagine, that Isaiah is thumbed far more than any other portion of the prophetical writings ; and this is due not only to the divinely evangelical character of his message, but also to the nobly human style of his language.* All the resources of poetry and eloquence are at his command. Every realm of nature ministers to his stores of imagery ; and his language ranges through every mode of beauty and sublimity, being sometimes like the pealing of silver bells, and sometimes like the crashing of avalanches, and sometimes like the songs of seraphim. He is generally supposed to have been a native of Jerusalem and to have spent his life within its walls. So identified, indeed, is he with it, that he is coming to be called Isaiah of Jerusalem ; and a recent expounder of his prophecies says that Jerusalem was more to him than Athens to Demosthenes, Rome to Juvenal, or Florence to Dante. But, at some period of his life, he must have had ample experience also of a country life ; because the aspects of the country are mirrored in his pages with incomparable charm.

He lets us see nature, as it existed in his day, both

---

* See the excellent chapter on Isaiah's style in Driver's *Isaiah.*

wild in the forest and wilderness, and cultivated around
the abodes of men ; and he paints for us the figures
of the country people themselves and the labours they
went forth to.   We see in his pages the trees of the
wood moved by the wind ; the willows by the water-
courses ; the fresh branches sprouting from the stock
of the pollard oak or terebinth.   We hear the doves
mourning from the depths of the thicket, and see the
roe, chased by the hunter, disappearing within its
shelter, and even the schoolboy rifling the birds' nests
so ruthlessly that " there was none that moved the
wing or opened the mouth or peeped."   We see the
swarms of bees and flies resting on the branches in
the summer heat ; the ploughshare lying in the furrow ;
the tow and the distaff ; the ox turning its head to
be patted by the hand of its owner, and the ass
trotting off at feeding-time to its master's crib.   The
prophet looks with a specially observant and sympathetic eye on the toils of men—the woodman thinning
the trees of the forest ; the carpenter, with saw and
axe, turning to his own uses the sycamore and the
cedar ; the builder among his bricks and stones ; and
the farmer, on the exposed height of the threshing-
floor, winnowing his corn with the shovel and the
fan.   As is usual in the Bible, the shepherd is pour-
trayed with special honour, whether he calls out his
neighbours to frighten away the lion from his flock

or is seen gathering the lambs in his arms and carrying them in his bosom. But most of all does the poet-prophet love to linger in the vineyard, marking accurately all the operations of the vine-dresser and all the stages of the growth of the vines. We see the tearing up of the hillside with the mattock, the accumulation of soil, the gathering out of the stones, the construction of the winepress and the watch-tower. Then we see the roots planted and growing from stage to stage—from that "afore the harvest, when the bud is perfect and the sour grape is ripening in the flower," to that when the vineyard is ringing with the songs of the vintage and the gleaners are picking the last relics from the outermost branches.

At whatever period these pictures of nature were laid up in the memory of Isaiah, they came back to him when he was engaged in the work of a prophet, and supplied the imagery by means of which the Divine truths which he heralded were made impressive and attractive to his countrymen and acceptable to all subsequent generations ; for men are so made that they are never so won by the truth as when they see it reflected in a physical image.

These two sides of the prophet's activity nearly correspond to what we should call Thought and Expression. Or, to put it still more broadly, the preacher must be a man who both has something to say and knows how to say it. On these two apparently simple qualifications hang all the science and art of our vocation.

In reality they are not simple. To have the right thing to say is a great commandment, and to know the right way to say it is, though second to it, hardly inferior. But the problem of the ministry is to have both in perfect equipoise—to utter a word which is at the same time both a message from God and a message to men.

It would be possible to be so taken possession of by the message from God as to lose self-control and even reason itself. In Scripture we meet with manifestations of prophecy which are akin to madness. Just as the wind, catching the sail, would, if the ropes were not adjusted to relieve the strain, overturn the boat, so the Wind of God might sweep the mind off its balance, the human personality being overborne by the inrushing inspiration. Thus religion may make a man a fanatic, who has no control over his own spirit, and no wisdom to choose the times at which to speak or the terms in which to address his fellow-men. On the other hand, the opposite excess is still more easy. So much stress may be laid on the form of words, and so much mastery obtained of the art of winning attention, that the necessity of having a Divine message to deliver or of depending on the power of the Spirit of God is forgotten. The windy master of words, whose own spirit is not subdued either by the impression of great thoughts or the sense of a great responsibility, but who can draw the eyes of men on his own performances and earn the incense of applause, has always been too familiar a figure in religion. It is to a man like Isaiah we must look for the absolute balance of both sides. There you have the blowing in all its degrees of the Wind of God, from the gentlest whisper to the force of the tempest, but, at the same time, the most perfect self-control and the adaptation of the word to the tastes and necessities of those to whom it was delivered.

There is a name sometimes applied by the prophets to themselves which admirably expresses the combination and balance of these two aspects of their activity. They call themselves Interpreters. The process of interpretation is a most interesting one, when it is well done. I have heard a speaker address with the greatest fervour a multitude who did not understand a word he was saying ; but, as fast as the sentences fell from his lips, another speaker by his side caught them up and, in tones as fervid and with gestures as dramatic as his own, rendered them to the hearers in their own tongue with such effect, that the performance made all the impression of an original speech. An interpreter is one who receives a message for people in a language which they do not understand and delivers it to them in their own tongue. Jehovah was incessantly speaking to His people in the vicissitudes of their history, but they did not apprehend His meaning. The prophet, however, understood ; he took the Divine message into his own soul, and then he went and communicated it to the people in terms with which they were familiar. An interpreter requires to know at least two languages —that in which the message comes and that in which it has to be delivered. If he knows either imperfectly, his interpretation will be proportionately imperfect. No interpreter of God, perhaps, knows both languages equally well. Some know the Divine language imperfectly, while they know thoroughly the language of men. What they say is interesting, fresh and human ; but there is not much of a Divine message in it. Others have got far into the secret of God and know the Divine language well ; but they are not sufficiently masters of the language of men. These are saintly men and command reverence by their character, but what they say does not find its way to men's business and bosoms.

I have seen the same truth put in another way. Tholuck, one of the most gifted of modern preachers, has made the remark, that a sermon ought to have heaven for its father and the earth for its mother. Why, he asks, do one half of our sermons miss the mark? It is because, while they treat of the circumstances and relationships of life in an interesting way, they do so only in the light which springs from below, not in that which streams from above : they have the earth for their mother, but not heaven for their father. And why do the other half of our sermons fail to touch the heart? It is because, while they display the heavenly things shining at a distance, they do not bring them down to the homes and workshops, the highways and byeways of ordinary life : they have heaven for their father, but not the earth for their mother.*

Indeed, gentlemen, the definition of the preacher as a Man of the Word covers a very large area of our duty, and an analysis of its contents will furnish a kind of natural history of that which is the most important part of a minister's work from week to week.

---

* The same idea has long been helpful to me in a third form—in the following lines of Platen—

> Was stets und aller Orten
> Sich ewig jung erweist
> Ist, in gebundenen Worten
> Ein ungebundener Geist.

1. To be a Man of the Word is to be a master of the Divine Word. In the pulpit not only must a man have something to say, but it must be a message from God. Where is this to be found? We do not now require to seek it, as the prophets had to do, in the empty void. Their work was not in vain. They were working for their own times, but they were also working for all time. The prophets and apostles put into a permanent form the principles on which the world is governed, and gave classical expression to the most important truths which man requires to know for salvation and for the conduct of his life. Thus they are still serving us, and we can begin where they left off. He who receives the message of God now finds it in the Word of God.

Hence one of the primary qualifications of the ministry is an intimate familiarity with the Scriptures. To this end a large proportion of the study required of you at college is directed ; and the subsequent habits of ministerial life have to be formed with the same object in view. A large portion of our work is the searching of the Scriptures, and a preacher of the highest order will always be a man mighty in the Scriptures. We chance at present to be living at a time when the questions about the Bible are the most numerous and the most difficult in theology, and many accepted opinions are cast into solution. I daresay it is the experience of most students of divinity that they are more perplexed about inspiration and related questions than about any other subjects. On the other hand, the attention directed to the Bible was never so great as it is at present ; and the methods of studying it are daily improving. And, in spite of all the difficulties, it is questionable if there ever was in the Church an intenser conviction that the voice of God is heard in His Word. The experience of the ministry deepens this conviction every year. If I may give utterance to my own experience, I have never come to the end of a close study of a book of Scripture in the congregation without having both a fresh respect for its literary character and a profounder impression of its Divine wisdom. The more the Bible is searched, the more will it be loved ; and the stronger will the conviction grow, that its deep truths are the Divine answers to the deep wants of human nature.

Yet to deliver the message of God is not merely to read what prophets and apostles penned and to repeat it by rote. The man who is to be God's messenger must himself draw near to God and abide in His secret, as they did. The word must detach itself from the book and become a living element of experience, before it can profit even the reader himself ; and much more is this the case, of course, before it can profit others.*   It is the truth which has become a personal conviction, and is burning in a man's heart so that he cannot be silent, which is his message. The number of such truths which a man has appropriated from the Bible and verified in his own experience is the measure of his power.†   There is all the difference in the world between the man who thus speaks what he knows from an inner impulse and the man whose sermon is simply a literary exercise on a Scripture theme, and who speaks only because Sunday has come round and the bell rung and he must do his duty.

The selection of the theme for preaching is to be determined chiefly by the power of the Word to lay hold of the conviction of the preacher.   Or, if the subject is prescribed, as when one is lecturing through

---

* " Into Ezekiel's hand there was put a roll written within and without with lamentation and mourning and woe, an objective revelation which he himself had not written ; but, before he could deliver it to others, he had to eat it : all that was written on it had to become a part of himself, had to be taken into his inmost experience and be digested by him, and become his own very life's blood."—MARCUS DODS, D.D.

† This is what our Lord chiefly meant by a teacher's " treasure "— " Every scribe which is instructed unto the kingdom of God bringeth forth out of his treasure things new and old."   How much the treasures of different preachers differ in magnitude !   It is worthy of note that the Saviour calls the preachers of the New Testament " scribes."   In spite of the evil associations of the name He retained it, because it emphasizes the fact that the Christian preacher is to be a student and an expounder of Scripture.

a book of the Bible, the points to be treated are to be determined in this way. Sometimes, as a preacher reads the Word, a text will leap from the page, so to speak, and, fastening on the mind, insist on being preached upon. A sermon on such a text is nearly always successful ; and a wise man will, therefore, take care to garner such texts when they occur to him. He will underline them in his Bible, or, better still, enter them in a note-book kept for the purpose, adding a few words perhaps to indicate the first lines of thought which have occurred to him. These notes may be multiplied from time to time ; and, when the minister turns to a page which has been thus filled, he will often find his sermon nearly made to his hand.* Dr. Wendell Holmes tells of Emerson that he kept such a note-book for subjects on which he might lecture, and for suggestions of lines of thought which he might follow out. He called it his Savings Bank, because, though the payments into it were minute, they gradually swelled to riches ; and passages which his hearers and readers supposed to be outbursts of sudden literary creation were really the results of slow accumulation. If this was necessary for even a genius like Emerson, it will be far more necessary

---

* Some preachers keep an interleaved Bible, in which references to passages in their reading are entered opposite the texts which they illustrate—an excellent device.

for the ordinary man. The gold of thought has generally to be collected as gold dust.

2. But this already brings me to the second stage of this natural history, which is, that the preacher must be a master of Human Words. The message from God which we carry is to become a message to men, and therefore we must know how to introduce it successfully to their notice. Strong as our own conviction may be, yet it may be crude and formless ; and, before it can become the conviction of others, it must take a shape which will arouse their attention. It may belong to a region of thought with which they are unfamiliar, and it has to be brought near, until it enters the circle of their own ideas.

This is the problem of the composition of the sermon, whether this means the writing of it out or the arrangement of the materials in the memory in preparation for delivery. And many rules might be given to help at this point.

One often recommended is to keep the audience in view to which the composition is to be addressed. If by this is meant that the writer, as he sits at his desk, should try to conjure up in his imagination the benches of the church and their occupants, I do not know whether it is a practicable rule or not. But, if it means that the preacher, as he composes his sermon, should keep in view the circumstances of his

hearers—their stage of culture, the subjects in which
they are interested, the Scriptural attainments which
they have already made, and the like—it is one of the
prime secrets of the preacher's art, and I will return
to speak of it more fully in a subsequent lecture. I
once heard Mr. Spurgeon preach a characteristic
sermon on an unusual text. It was on these words
in Hosea : " I was unto them as they that take off
the yoke on their jaws, and I laid meat unto them."
To illustrate the first clause he drew a graphic picture
of a London carter in Cornhill loosening the harness,
when his horse had surmounted the incline, taking
the bit out of its mouth, and fastening on the corn-
bag ; and he applied the second clause with humorous
wisdom to the behaviour of preachers. As the carter
in the stable " lays " the hay to his horse, so the
preacher has to " lay " the food to the congregation.
The carter must not put the food too high, where the
horse cannot reach up to it, nor too low, where it
cannot get down to it, but just where it can seize and
devour it with comfort. So the preacher must neither
pitch his message too high, where it will be above
the comprehension of the congregation, nor too low,
where it will not command their respect, but just
where they can reach it easily and comfortably. This
quaint illustration has often recurred to me in the
study, and made me anxiously consider whether I

8

was putting the truth in such a way that the congregation could grasp it.

Many rules have been proposed for winning the attention of the congregation. Some have laid stress on commencing the sermon with something striking. Mr. Moody, the evangelist, whose opinion on such a subject ought to be valuable, recommends the preacher to crowd in his best things at the beginning, when the attention is still fresh. Others have favoured the opposite procedure. During the first half of the discourse nearly every audience will give the speaker a chance. At this point, therefore, the heavier and drier things which need to be said ought to occur. But about the middle of the discourse the attention begins to waver. Here, therefore, the more picturesque and interesting things should begin to come ; and the very best should be reserved for the close, so that the impression may be strongest at the last.* St. Augustine says that a discourse should instruct, delight and convince ;† and perhaps these three impressions

---

* "The strongest part of all great sermons is the close. More depends on the last two minutes than on the first ten."—From a choice little tract on Preaching, by " Prediger."

† He is quoting Cicero. Dixit ergo quidam eloquens, et verum dixit, ita dicere debere eloquentem, ut doceat, ut delectet, ut flectat. Deinde addidit : Docere necessitatis est, delectare suavitatis, flectere victoriæ . . . Oportet igitur eloquentem ecclesiasticum, quando suadet aliquid quod agendum est, non solum docere ut instruat, et delectare ut teneat, verum etiam flectere ut vincat.—*De Doctrina Christiana*, IV. 13.

should, upon the whole, follow this order. The more instructive elements—the facts and explanations—should come first, appealing to the intellect; then should follow the illustrative and pathetic elements, which touch the feelings; and then, at the close, should come those moving and overawing considerations which stir the conscience and determine the will. Thus the impression would grow from the commencement to the close.*

To obtain command of language it is good to hear the best speakers and to read the best books. It has been my fortune to be acquainted with a good many celebrated preachers; and I have observed that, almost without exception, they have had a thorough acquaintance with the whole range of the higher English literature. To have the music of Shakspeare or Milton echoing in your memory, or

---

* An esteemed friend, the Rev. John McMillan of Ullapool, some years ago repeated to me the following rhyme on the method of constructing a sermon, and, although I have never succeeded in coming up to its standard, yet it has often floated before me with advantage in the hours of composition—

> " Begin low ;
> Proceed slow ;
> Rise higher ;
> Take fire ;
> When most impressed
> Be self-possessed ;
> To spirit wed form ;
> Sit down in a storm."

to have lingering in your ear the cadence and sweep of the sentences of Thackeray and De Quincey, will almost unawares give you a good style.* In reading over an old sermon of my own, I can almost tell whether or not, in the week of its composition, I was reading good literature. In the former case the language is apt to be full and harmonious, and sprinkled over with gay flowers of maxim and illustration, whereas in the latter the style of the performance is apt to be bald and jerky.†

Let me mention one more rule for the composition of the sermon which appears to me to be the most important of all. It is, to take time. Begin in time and get done in time—this, I often say to myself, is the whole duty of a minister. The reason why so many of our sermons are crude in thought, unbalanced in the arrangement of the materials, destitute of literary beauty, and unimpressive in delivery, is because they are begun too late and written too

---

* It will be remembered that John Bright used regularly, during the session of Parliament, to read aloud from one of the poets the last thing at night.

† Tholuck gives another weighty reason why ministers should know the best literature : In einer Zeit wo Shakespeare eine stärkere Autorität für Viele ist als Paulus, und ein Distichon Göthes eine kräftigere Belegstelle als der ganze Römer-und Galaterbrief, darf der Geistliche, welcher auf seine Gemeinde würken will, mit ihren Gewährsmännern nicht unbekannt seyn. Wenn irgendwo, so gilt auch hier des Apostels Wort : *Alles ist Euer.*

hurriedly. The process of thinking especially should be prolonged ; it is not so important that the process of writing should be slow. It is when the subject has been long tossed about in thought that the mind begins to glow about it ; the subject itself gets hot and begins to melt and flash, until at last it can be poured forth in a facile but glowing stream. Style is not something added to the thought from the outside. It is simply the beauty of the truth itself, when you have gone deep enough to find it ; and the worst condemnation of a careless and unattractive style is that it does the truth injustice.

3. The preacher ought to be master of the Oral Word. There is a stage which the truth has to pass through after it has been prepared in the study for the consumption of the hearers. This is the oral delivery ; and it is a part of the natural history of the sermon which must not be overlooked. A sermon may be well composed in the study and yet be a failure in the pulpit. Indeed, this is one of the most critical stages of the entire process. There are few things more disappointing than to have received a message to deliver and spent a laborious and happy week in composition, and yet on Sunday, as you descend the pulpit stair, to know that you have missed the mark. This, however, is far from an infrequent occurrence. The same sermon may even

be a success on one occasion, and on another a partial or a total failure.

Wherein a good delivery consists it is difficult to say. It is the rekindling of the fire of composition in the presence of the congregation ; it is the power of thinking out the subject again on your feet. This must not be a mere repetition of a byegone process, but a new and original action of the mind on the spot. Tholuck, to whom I have already alluded in this lecture, says that a sermon needs to be born twice : it must be born once in the study in the process of composition, and it must be born again in the pulpit in the process of delivery. Many a sermon is a genuine birth of the mind in the study which in the pulpit is still-born.*

Some preachers have an extraordinary facility of putting themselves at once, and every time, *en rapport* with the audience, so that there is from first to last, whilst they speak, a commerce between the mind in

---

* " Aber nicht bloss die Erzeugung der Predigt geschehe im heiligen Geist, sondern auch ihr Vortrag. Es lässt sich nicht aussprechen, welch' ein Unterschied zwischen der Würkung einer Predigt, welche bloss aus der Erinnerung von der Kanzel herabgesprochen wird—wie trefflich sie auch übrigens seyn mag—und welche dort zum zweitenmal geboren wird in lebendigem Glauben. . . . Die Predigt muss eine That des Predigers auf zeinem Studirzimmer, sie muss abermals eine That seyn auf der Kanzel ; er muss, wenn er herunter kommt, Mutterfreuden fühlen, Freuden der Mutter, die unter Gottes Segen ein Kind geborei hat."

the pulpit and the minds in the pews. To others this is the most difficult part of preaching. The difficulty is to get down amongst the people and to be actually dealing with them. Many a preacher has a thought, and is putting it into good enough words, but somehow the people are not listening, and they cannot listen.

If the Senate of this University were ever to try the experiment of asking a layman to deliver this course of Lectures on Preaching, I am certain he would lay more stress on this than we do, and put a clear and effective—if possible, a graceful and eloquent —delivery among the chief desiderata of the pulpit. I do not know how it may be among you ; but, when I was at college, we used rather to despise delivery. We were so confident in the power of ideas that we thought nothing of the manner of setting them forth. Only have good stuff, we thought, and it will preach itself. We liked to repeat, with *Faust,*

> True sense and reason reach their aim
> With little help from art and rule ;
> Be earnest ! then what need to seek
> The words that best your meaning speak ?

So we thought ; and many of us have since suffered for it. We know how many sermons are preached in the churches of the country every Sunday ; but does anyone know how many are listened to ? The newspapers supply us now and then with statistics of how many hearers are present in our congregations; but who will tell us what proportion of these are listeners? If we knew the exact percentage, I suspect, it would appal us. Yet it is not because there is not good matter in the sermons, but because it is not properly spoken. In the manufacture of steam-engines the problem is, I believe, to get as much work as possible out of the coal consumed. In every engine which has ever yet been constructed there has been a greater or less waste of heat, which is dispersed into the surrounding air or carried away by the adjacent portions of the machinery, without doing work. Engineering skill has been gradually reducing the amount of this waste and getting a larger and larger proportion of work out of the fuel; and a perfect engine would be one in which the whole of the coal consumed had its full equivalent in work done. One of our problems, it seems to me, is a similar one. There is an enormous disproportion between the amount of energy expended during the week in preparation and the amount of impression made on the hearers on Sunday. Ministers do not get enough of result in the attention, satisfaction and delight of their hearers for the work they do; and the failure is in the vehicle of communication between the study and the congregation—that is to say, in the delivery of the sermon. What I am pleading for is, that there should be more work to show for the coal consumed.*

4. Allow me, gentlemen, in closing this lecture, to emphasize another sense in which the prophets were men of the Word, and in which they are worthy of

---

* Adolphe Monod, himself a distinguished master of the art of delivery, gives some good hints on it in a paper on " The Eloquence of the Pulpit," translated and published as an article in *The British and Foreign Evangelical Review*, January 1881 :—

" In general, people recite too quickly, far too quickly. When a man speaks, the thoughts and feelings do not come to him all at once ; they take birth little by little in his mind. It is necessary that this labour and this slowness appear in the reciting, or it will always come short of nature. Take time to reflect, to feel, and to allow ideas to come, and hurry your recitation only when constrained by some particular consideration." . . .

" Talk not in the pulpit. An exaggerated familiarity would be a mistake nearly as great as declamation : it happens more seldom ; it is, nevertheless, found in certain preachers, those especially who have not studied. The tone of good conversation, but that tone heightened and ennobled, such appears to me the ideal of pulpit delivery." . . .

" In order to rise above the tone of conversation, the majority of preachers withdraw too far from it. They swell their delivery, and declaim instead of speaking. Now, when bombast comes in, nature goes out."

In regard to the first of these extracts I should say that many Scotch speakers fail through lack of *pace* in the delivery. The interest is lost in the pauses between the sentences. A slow delivery is only effective when a thought is obviously being born, for which the audience is kept intently waiting.

But the most remarkable thing in the article is the following quota-tion from Talma, the actor :—

" We were rhetoricians and not characters. What scores of aca-demical discourses on the theatre, how few simple words ! But by

imitation.   They were masters of the Written Word.
They not only spoke the word of God, but wrote
it for publication, in a form sometimes more diffuse
and sometimes more compressed than their oral
utterances ; and by this means they not only
extended their influence in their own day, but have
enormously prolonged it since.

It is surprising how few of those who have spoken

chance I found myself one evening in a drawing-room with the
leaders of the party of the Gironde.   Their sombre countenance, their
anxious look, attracted my attention.   There were there, written in
visible letters, strong and powerful interests.   They were men of
too much heart for those interests to be tarnished by selfishness ; I
saw in them the manifest proof of the danger of my country.   All
come to enjoy pleasure ; not one thinking of it !   They began to
discuss ; they touched on the most thrilling questions of the day.   It
was grand !   Methought I was attending one of the secret councils
of the Romans.   'The Romans must have spoken like these,' said I.
'Let the country be called France or Rome, it makes use of the
same intonations, speaks the same language : therefore, if there is no
declamation here before me, there was no declamation down there, in
olden times ; that is evident !'   These reflections rendered me more
attentive.   My impressions, though produced by a conversation
thoroughly free from bombast, deepened.   'An apparent calm in men
agitated stirs the soul,' said I ; 'eloquence may then have strength,
without the body yielding to disordered movements.'   I even perceived
that the discourse, when delivered without efforts or cries, renders the
gesture more powerful and gives the countenance more expression.
All these deputies assembled before me by chance appear to me much
more eloquent in their simplicity than at the tribune, where, being in
spectacle, they think they must deliver their harangue in the way of
actors—and actors as we were then—that is, declaimers, full of
bombast.   From that day a new light flashed on me ; I foresaw my art
regenerated."

the word of God have cultivated this mode of delivering it ; and it is perhaps equally astonishing how few of those who have cultivated it have done so in earnest. In last century, promotion in the Church of England was won by literary achievement ; but the would-be bishop did not generally think of religious literature : he published a political pamphlet or edited a Greek play. Among the Scottish Moderates there was a keen ambition for literary distinction ; but it was the more prized the more remote the fields in which it was won lay from a minister's peculiar work. This led the Evangelicals to discountenance literary productivity, which they regarded as springing from unholy motives and as likely to distract the mind from the true ends of the ministry. But surely there is a juster point of view than either the Moderate or the Evangelical. This work ought to be cultivated with precisely the same aims as preaching and with the same earnestness. When a man is truly called to it, it brings a vast audience within his range, and there may rest on it a remarkable blessing. Here is a significant extract from the history of British Christianity : Richard Baxter wrote *A Call to the Unconverted*, and Philip Doddridge was converted by reading it ; Philip Doddridge wrote *The Rise and Progress of Religion in the Soul*, and William Wilberforce was converted by reading it ; Wilberforce wrote

The *Practical View*, and Thomas Chalmers was converted by reading it.   What a far-extending influence
does each of these names represent!   The writing of
books is perhaps the likeliest of all avenues by which
to carry religious influence to the most select minds.[*]

---

[*] Referring to this subject, Schleiermacher, in his *Praktische Theologie*,
makes the following characteristic remark : "Das ist eben das grosse
und vortreffliche was allen freien Gemeinschaften eigen ist, ganz
vorzüglich aber der christlichen Kirche, die ihre Berechnung hat auf
das ganze menschliche Geschlecht, ganz besonders aber der freien
Gestaltung derselben in unserer evangelischen Kirche, dass einem
jeden in dem Masse, wie ihm das geistige Auge geöffnet ist, eine
Wirksamkeit auf das Ganze der Kirche sich eröffnet, und dass man es
einer jeden Wirksamkeit anmerken kann, in wie fern eines dem Geiste
nach der grossen Gemeinschaft angehört, oder ob er freiwillig sich
davon ausgeschlossen hat und aus dem Gesichtspunkt eines kleinen
Gebietes wirkt."

V.

THE PREACHER AS A FALSE PROPHET

LECTURE V.

THE PREACHER AS A FALSE PROPHET.

UPON anyone who is studying the physiognomy of the age of the prophets there is one disagreeable feature which obtrudes itself so constantly that even in the briefest sketch it is impossible to pass it by. This is the activity of the false prophets.* It culminated in the lifetime of Jeremiah, whose whole career might almost be described as a conflict with them. Again and again he and they came to open war ; and on at least one occasion the whole body combined to take away his life. Ezekiel was scarcely less afflicted by them. They were perhaps

---

* As this subject is somewhat novel, the following collection of texts may be acceptable ; but it is not given as exhaustive :—

Isa. ii. 6; xxviii. 7 ; xxx. 10, 11 ; xlvii. 13 ; lvi. 10-12.

Jer. ii. 8, 26; iv. 9 ; v. 31 ; vi. 14; xiv. 13-16 ; xviii. 18 ; xxiii. 9-40 (*locus classicus*) ; xxvi. 8 ; xxvii. 9, 16 ; xxviii. xxix. 8.

Ezek. xii. 24; xiii. (*locus classicus*) ; xiv. 9 ; xx. 25; xxi. 23 ; xxii. 25, 28.

Micah ii. 11 ; iii. 5, 11.

Zeph. iii, 4.

Zech. x. 2 ; xiii. 2-4.

not so prominent an element in the life of Isaiah, but he also refers to them frequently; and, indeed, their sinister figures haunt the pages of all the prophets.

It is a kind of humiliation to speak of them at all, and I would gladly pass them by; but the figure of the true prophet will rise before our eyes more clearly by the contrast of the false : and it is perhaps a duty to look also at the degradations to which our office is liable. The higher the honour attaching to the ministerial profession, when it is worthily filled, the deeper is the abuse of which it is capable in comparison with other callings; and its functions are so sacred that the man who discharges them must either be a man of God or a hypocrite. Yet there are plenty of motives of an inferior kind which may take the place of right ministerial aims. Though it is painful to speak of such things, yet here again the method which we have adopted in these lectures, of following the guidance of Scripture, may be leading us better than we could have chosen ourselves ; and it may be wholesome to have to look at an aspect of our subject which of our own accord we would avoid.

There are two things in Scripture which I have never been able to think of without strong movements of fear and self-distrust.

One of them is that, when the Son of God came to this earth, He was persecuted and slain by the religious classes. His deadly opponents were the Scribes and Pharisees. But who were the Scribes and Pharisees ? The Scribes occupied almost exactly the position in the community which is held among us by the literary, the scholastic and the clerical classes ; and the Pharisees were simply what we should now call the leading religious laymen. Had they been adherents of a false religion, there would have been nothing surprising in their resistance to the final revelation of the true God. But the religion which they professed was the true religion ; the Scribes were the expounders of the Word of God, and the Pharisees occupied the foremost places in the house of God. Yet, when the Son of Jehovah, whose name they were called by, appeared amongst them, they rejected Him and took away His life. Many a time, as I have followed Jesus step by step through His lifelong conflict with their illwill and contradiction, the question has pressed itself painfully upon my mind : If He were to come to the earth now and intervene in our affairs, how would the religious classes receive Him ? and on which side would I be myself ? If to any this question may seem fantastic, let them change it into this other, which cannot appear idle, though it means exactly

9

the same thing : What is the attitude of the religious classes to the manifestations of the spirit of Jesus in the life of to-day? do they welcome them and back them up? or have the new ideas and movements in which Christ is marching onward to the conquest of the world to reckon on opposition, even from those who call themselves most loudly by His name?

The other circumstance which has often affected my mind in the same way is that which comes before us to-day—that the true prophets of the Old Testament had to face the opposition, not of heathens, and not of the openly irreligious among their own countrymen only, but of those who had the name of God in their mouths and were publicly recognised as His oracles.   To us these are now false prophets, because time has found them out and the Word of God has branded them with the title they deserve ; but in their own day they were regarded as true prophets ; and doubtless many of them never dreamed that they were not entitled to the name.

They must have been a numerous and powerful body.   Jeremiah mentions them again and again along with the king, the princes and the priests, as if they formed a fourth estate in the realm ; and Zephaniah mentions them in the same way along with the princes, the judges and the priests.   They evidently formed a separate and conspicuous class in the community. They cannot have been equally bad in every generation ; and there may have been many degrees of deviation among them from the character of the true prophet ; but as a body they were false, and the true servants of God had to reckon them among the anti-religious forces which they had to overcome.

This is an appalling fact—that the public representatives of religion should ever have been the worst enemies of religion ; but it cannot be denied that even in Christendom, and that not once or twice, the same condition of things has existed.

At the time these men did not suppose that this was the position they held ; but history has judged them. It is not easy for a man to admit the thought into his own mind that in him his office is being dishonoured and its aim frustrated ; and it is far more difficult to do so if he has the support of the prevailing sentiment and is going forward triumphantly as a member of the majority. But there is enough in the history of our order to warn us to watch over ourselves with a jealous mind, lest we too, while clad in the garb of a sacred profession and in the authority of an ecclesiastical position, should be found fighting against God. It will not do to think that, merely because we sit in Moses' seat and have the Word of God in our mouths, therefore we must be right. Nor must we be too confident because we are in the majority. If we have faith in our own views, it is quite right, indeed, that we should try to make them prevail ; and there is a legitimate joy in seeing a good cause carrying with it the sympathies and suffrages of men. But we are all too easily persuaded that our cause is good simply because it can win votes. In ecclesiastical affairs there is often as feverish a counting of heads as in party politics. The majority have the same confidence that the case is finally decided in their favour ; and there is the same exultation over the defeated party, as if their being in the minority were a clear proof that they were also in the wrong. But this is no criterion, and time may sternly reverse the victory of the moment. Even in the Church the side of the false prophets may be the growing and the winning side, while Jeremiah is left in a minority of one.

The false prophets were strong, not only in their own numbers, but in their popularity with the people. This told heavily against the true prophets ; for the people could not believe that the one man, who was standing alone, was right, and that his opponents, who were many, were wrong. The seats and the trappings of office always affect the multitude, who are slow to come to the conclusion that the teachers under whom they find themselves in providence can be misleading them. This is, to a certain extent, an honourable sentiment ; but it throws upon public teachers a weighty responsibility. If they are going wrong, they will generally get the majority of the people to follow them. So completely may this be the case, that by degrees the popular taste is vitiated and will not endure any other teaching than that to which it has been accustomed, though it be false. There is no sadder verse in all prophecy than the complaint of Jeremiah, "The prophets prophesy falsely, and My people love to have it so." Like prophet, like people ; the public mind may be so habituated to what is false, and satisfied with it, that it has no taste or even tolerance for the true.* Jeremiah could not gain a hearing for his stern and weighty message from ears accustomed to the light and frivolous views of the false prophets ; and to Baruch, his young coadjutor and amanuensis, who was starting on the prophetic career with the high hopes of youth, he had to deliver the chilling message, "Seekest thou great things for thyself? seek them not." The path to popularity and eminence was not open to anyone who did not speak according to the prevailing fashion.

---

* "Sicut autem cuius pulchrum corpus et deformis est animus, magis dolendus est, quam si deforme haberet et corpus, ita qui eloquenter ea quæ falsa sunt dicunt, magis miserandi sunt, quam si talia deformiter dicerent."—ST. AUGUSTINE,

The false prophets won and kept their popularity by pandering to the opinions and prejudices of the people. The times of Jeremiah were big with coming calamities, and he had to predict that these calamities were sure to come ; for there were no signs of deep or genuine repentance, and, indeed, the time for repentance was past. The self-flattering, ease-loving people hated to hear these disagreeable facts. Their frivolous minds were engrossed with the gossip and excitement of the passing day, and it was too great an exertion to give their attention to the majestic views of the Divine justice and the far-reaching sweep of the Divine providence to which Jeremiah tried to direct their attention. They wished to enjoy the present and to believe that all would come right somehow. The false prophets flattered these wishes. They said that the calamities which Jeremiah was foretelling would not come to pass, or that at least they would be much less formidable than he represented. They were, as Jeremiah says, like an unconscientious physician, who is afraid to probe the wound to the bottom, though the life of the patient depends on it. Ezekiel accuses them of making nightcaps to draw over the eyes and ears of their countrymen, lest they should see and hear the truth, and of muffling with a glove the naked hand of God with which the sins of the people should have been smitten. The constant refrain of their prophecies was, " Peace, peace," though the storm-clouds of retribution were ready to burst. The people said to them, " Prophesy to us smooth things"; and the false prophets provided the supply according to the demand.

We cannot flatter ourselves that this is a danger which belongs entirely to the past. There will always be a demand for smooth things, and an appropriate reward for him who is willing to supply them in the name of God. Popularity is a thing which will always be coveted ; and under certain conditions it is a thing to be thankful for. If it means that the truth is prevailing and that men are yielding their minds to its sway, it is a precious gift of heaven. It is a good thing to see many coming out to hear the Word of God, and to both preacher and hearers there is a great deal of exhilaration and inspiration in a full church. But popularity may be purchased at too dear a rate. It may be bought by the suppression of the truth and the letting down of the demands of Christianity. There will always be a demand for a religion which does not agitate the mind too much or interfere with the pursuits of a worldly life.

I have seen a very trenchant article from an American pen on the power of the moneyed members of a church to dictate the tone of the pulpit ; and it

is a common accusation against ministers, that they
flatter the prevailing classes in their congregations.
If their congregations are wealthy, they are afraid, it
is said, to speak up for the poor, even when justice is
calling out on their side ; and, if their congregations
are poor, they take the side of the working-man, right
or wrong.   I should question whether temptations so
gross as these are much felt.   Far more dangerous
are the subtler temptations—to truckle to the spirit
of the age, to keep at all hazards on the side of the
cultivated and clever, and to shun those truths the
utterance of which might expose the teacher to the
charge of being antiquated and bigoted.   Let a
preacher dwell always on the sunny side of the truth
and conceal the shadows, let him enlarge continually
on what is simple and human in Christianity and pass
lightly over what is mysterious and Divine : let him,
for example, dwell on the human side of Christ but
say nothing of His deity, let him enforce Christ's
example but say nothing of His atonement, let him
extol the better elements of human nature but say
nothing of its depravity, let him preach frequently on
the glories of the next world but never mention its
terrors : and very probably he may be popular and see
his church crowded ; but he will be a false prophet.*

* Even popularity honestly won may be a great snare. Vanity, it
must be allowed, is probably the commonest clerical weakness ; and,

Who were these false prophets, and how did there come to be such numbers of them? These are questions which an attentive reader of the Bible cannot help asking; but it is not by any means easy to answer them.

The prophets whose names have come down to us are not by any means numerous; but, besides them, there must have been many other true prophets.

---

when it is yielded to, it deforms the whole character. There are few things more touching or instructive than the entries in Dr. Chalmers' journal, which show with what earnestness he was praying against this, in the height of his popularity, as a besetting sin. If this were common, there would not be the slight accent of contempt attached to the name of the popular preacher which now belongs to it in the mouths of men. The publicity which beats on the pulpit makes veracity, down to the bottom of the soul, more necessary in the clerical than in any other calling. "A prime virtue in the pulpit is mental integrity. The absence of it is a subtle source of moral impotence. It concerns other things than the blunt antipodes represented by a truth and a lie. Argument which does not satisfy a preacher's logical instinct; illustration which does not commend itself to his æsthetic taste; a perspective of doctrine which is not true to the eye of his deepest insight; the use of borrowed materials which offend his sense of literary equity; an emotive intensity which exaggerates his conscious sensibility; an impetuosity of delivery which overworks his thought; gestures and looks put on for scenic effect; an eccentric elocution, which no *human* nature ever fashioned; even a shrug of the shoulder, thought of and planned for beforehand—these are causes of enervation in sermons which may be otherwise well framed and sound in stock. They sap a preacher's personality and neutralise his magnetism. They are not true, and he knows it. Hearers may know nothing of them theoretically, yet may feel the full brunt of their negative force practically."—AUSTIN PHELPS, D.D., *My Note Book.*

There were times when the spirit of religion was breathing through the community, and then men were not wanting who felt called to be its organs. The spirit of inspiration might fall on any one at any time ; no prescribed training was necessary to make a man a prophet. It might come, as it did to Amos, on the husbandman in his fields or the shepherd among his flock. It might alight on the young noble amidst the opening pleasures of life, as it did on Isaiah and Zephaniah ; or it might come, as it did on Jeremiah and Ezekiel, on the young priest preparing for his sacred functions.

But some of the more noted prophets endeavoured in a more systematic way to diffuse the spirit which rested upon themselves, and thus to multiply the number of the prophets. They founded schools in which promising young men were gathered and plied with the means of education available in that age, cultivating music, reading the writings of the older prophets, and coming under the influence of the holy man who was at their head. These were the Schools of the Prophets, and their students were the Sons of the Prophets. Samuel seems to have been the first founder of these schools. They were flourishing in the times of Elijah and Elisha, and they probably continued to exist with varying fortunes in subsequent centuries. Perhaps all who went through these schools claimed, or could claim, the prophetic name. Those who took up the profession wore the hairy mantle and leathern girdle made familiar to us by the figure of John the Baptist; and they probably subsisted on the gifts of those who benefited from their oracles. Their numbers may have been very large; we hear of hundreds of prophets even during an idolatrous reign, when they were exposed to persecution.

In times when the spirit of inspiration was abroad or when the schools enjoyed the presence of a master spirit, it is easy to understand how valuable such institutions may have been, and how they may have been centres from which religious light and warmth were diffused through the whole country. But they were liable to deterioration. If the general tone of religion in the country declined, they partook in the general decay; an inspiring leader might be taken away and no like-minded successor arise to fill his place; or men who had received no real call beforehand might join the school and pass through the curriculum without receiving it. Only they had learned the trick of speech and got by rote the language of religion. They had no personal knowledge of God or message obtained directly from Him; but it was not difficult to put on the prophet's mantle and talk in the traditional prophetic tones. The fundamental charge against the false prophets is always this: " I have not sent these prophets, yet they ran ; I have not spoken unto them, yet they prophesy."

If I am right in tracing the origin of false prophecy to the schools of the prophets, this gives a suggestive hint as to the point at which the same danger may beset ourselves. It is obviously the duty of the authorities of the Church to make provision for the training of those who are to be the future ministers of the Gospel ; and it is natural for those who have the honour of the Church at heart to covet for her service the talents of the gifted. Parents, too, will often be found cherishing an intense desire that the choicest of their sons should become ministers. These wishes of superiors have a legitimate influence in determining the choice of our life-work. The wishes and prayers of pious parents are especially entitled to have very great weight. Yet there is a danger of an outward influence of this kind being substituted for genuine personal experience and an inward call. When, a generation ago, in the rural parts of England, the church in many a parish was looked upon as " a living," to be allocated to a junior member of the family, who was educated for the position as a matter of course, the custom, whatever happy results it might produce in exceptional cases, was not fitted to fill the pulpits of the land with men of prophetic character. The pious wishes of parents, however beautiful they may be, require to be made absolutely conditional on a vocation of a higher kind ; otherwise we get a manufactured ministry, without a message, in place of men in whom the spirit of inspiration is stirring and who speak because they believe.

Having no message of their own, what were the false prophets to do? The best they could do was to repeat and imitate what had been said by their predecessors. It is with this Jeremiah reproaches them when he says, "Behold, I am against the prophets, saith the Lord, that steal My words every-one from his neighbour." The older prophets used to begin their utterances with the phrase, "the burden of the Lord ;" and Jeremiah complains that this had become an odious cant term in the mouths of his contemporaries ; and in the same way Zechariah complains that in his day the great word " comfort," which from the lips of Isaiah had descended like dew from heaven on the parched hearts of the people of God, had become a dry and hackneyed phrase in the mouths of false prophets. How dangerous this habit of stealing the words of others might become, when practical issues were involved, may be illustrated by a striking example. The inviolability of Jerusalem had been a principle of the older prophets, which was quite true for their times ; and Isaiah had made use of it for rousing his fellow-citizens from despair, when the army of Sennacherib stood before the gates. But in Jeremiah's time the change of circumstances had made it to be no longer true ; and yet the false prophets kept on repeating it ; and no doubt they seemed both to themselves and others to be occupying a strong position when, in opposing him, they could allege that they were standing on the same ground as Isaiah. All the time, however, they were betraying those who listened to them.

There is a sense in which the truth of God is unchangeable ; it is like Himself—the same yesterday and to-day and forever. But there is another sense in which it is continually changing. Like the manna, it descends fresh every morning, and, if it is kept till to-morrow, it breeds loathsome worms. Isaiah describes the true prophet as one who has the tongue of the learner—not of the learned, as the Authorised Version gives it—and whose ear is opened every morning to hear the message of the new day. What was truth for yesterday may be falsehood for to-day ; and only he is a trustworthy interpreter of God who is sensitive to the indications of present providence.

It would, however, be a mistake to suppose that the only form which false prophecy can take is a dried-up orthodoxy, mumbling over the shibboleths of yesterday. If he who stands forward as a speaker for God is out of touch with God and has really no Divine message, he may make good the lack of a true Divine word in many ways. The easiest way is, no doubt, to fall back on some accepted word of yesterday; but he may also strike out on the path of originality, announcing a gospel for to-morrow, constructed by his own fancy, which has no Divine sanction. Neither orthodoxy nor heterodoxy is a guarantee: the only guarantee is a humble mind living in the secret of the Lord.

I have mentioned that the prophets subsisted on the contributions of those to whom their oracles were supposed to be valuable. There is, indeed, very little information on this head; but they are accused of prophesying for bread, and avarice and a greedy appetite for the good things of this life are reproaches frequently cast at them. It is not likely that prophecy can ever have been a paying profession, but it would appear to have been at least a means of livelihood; and there are indications that those who enjoyed an exceptional popularity may have occupied a high social standing. Ezekiel, whose characterizations of the false prophets are remarkably striking, uses about them a significant figure of speech. He says that, while a true prophet was like a wall of fire to his country, standing in the breach when danger threatened and defending it with his life, the false prophets were like the foxes that burrow among the ruins of fallen cities. What mattered it to them that their country was degraded, if only they had found comfortable places for themselves?

This also is a painful side of the subject. It is inevitable that the ministry should become a means of livelihood, and yet it is fatal to pursue it with this in view. It is the least lucrative of the professions, and yet, in the pressure of modern life, it may tempt men to join it merely as a profession. Even if it has been entered upon from higher motives, the attrition of domestic necessities may dry up the nobler motives and convert the minister into a hireling who thinks chiefly of his wages.* The commercial spirit is omnipotent in our day ; and men who can buy everything

---

* " That which in its idea is the divinest of earthly employments has necessarily come to be also a profession, a line of life, with its routine, its commonplace, its poverty and deterioration of motive, its coarseness of feeling. It cannot but be so. It is part of the conditions of our mortality. Even earnest purpose, even zealous and laborious service, cannot alone save from the lowered tone and dulness of spirit which are our insensible but universal and inveterate enemies in all the business of real life. And that torpor and insensibility and deadness to what is high and great is, more than any other evil, the natural foe of all that is characteristic and essential in the Christian ministry ; for that ministry is one of life and reality, or it is nothing."—DEAN CHURCH.

for money think that ministers are procurable in the same way. Thus they tempt men away with bribes of money from work to which God has called them. I am far from questioning the importance of the mission of the pulpit to the wealthier classes; and we must have men of culture to preach to the cultivated. I would no more think of setting up the poor against the rich, as the exclusive objects of the Church's attention, than the rich against the poor. But perhaps the most essential work of the Church at the present time is to win and to hold the working-classes. I should like to see ministers coveting work among them; and let him who has learned to wield such an audience, where he can speak with the freedom and force of nature, beware of being bribed away to a position where he will be tamed and domesticated, and have his teeth drawn and his claws cut.

So monotonous is the evil side of the false prophets that one longs for a gleam of something good in them. Can they not at least be pitied? May they not have been weak men, who were elevated to a position which proved too much for them? The times were full of change and difficulty, and it required a clear eye to see the indications of Providence. It is not every one who has the genius of an Isaiah or the magnificent moral courage of a Jeremiah

10

Was it not possible to take a milder view of the world than Jeremiah did, and yet be a true man? May they not at least have been mistaken, when they ventured to emit prophecies which history falsified?

Such sentiments easily arise in us; but they are driven back by what we read of the personal character of these men. "Both prophet and priest," says Jeremiah, "are profane; yea, in My house have I found their wickedness, saith the Lord." "I have seen," he says in God's name, "in the prophets of Jerusalem an horrible thing: they commit adultery and walk in lies." Jeremiah's view of them might be thought to be coloured by his own melancholy temperament; but Isaiah's is not less severe: "The priest and the prophet," he says, "have erred through wine, they are swallowed up of wine, they are out of the way through strong drink." And he gives this terrible picture of them: "His watchmen are blind, they are ignorant; they are all dumb dogs, they cannot bark; sleeping, lying down, loving to slumber. Yea, they are greedy dogs which can never have enough, and they are shepherds that cannot understand; they all look to their own way, every one to his gain from his quarter. Come ye, say they, I will fetch wine, and we will fill ourselves with strong drink; and to-morrow shall be as this day and still more abundant." The representations in the other prophets are to the same effect. Zephaniah passes on the whole class the sweeping judgment, that they are light and treacherous persons. But the lowest deep is reached in Zechariah, who foresees a time, close at hand, when the very name of prophet will be a byword, and the father and mother of anyone who pretends to prophesy, will thrust him through, to deliver themselves from the reproach of having any connection with him.*

The influence of such a travesty of the sacred office as these passages describe must have been deplorable ; and without doubt it was one of the principal causes of the overthrow of the Jewish State. Jeremiah says expressly, that from the prophets profaneness had gone out over the whole land. They who, from their position and profession, ought to have been an example to their fellow-countrymen were the very reverse. They were the companions of the profane and licentious in their revels, and they joined with scorners in scoffing at those who led a strict and holy life. So God charges them by the lips of Ezekiel : "Ye have made the hearts of the righteous sad, whom I have not made sad, and

---

* This may perhaps help to determine the age of the portion of Zechariah to which this passage belongs. Is there any proof elsewhere that a degradation of the prophetic office as deep as this had taken place, or was imminent, at the period to which it is usually assigned ?

strengthened the hands of the wicked, that he should not return from his wicked way."

This is a terrible picture. Yet there have been epochs in the history of the Christian, and even of the Protestant Church, when its features have been reproduced with too faithful literality. Let us be thankful that we live in a happier time; but let us also remember the maxim, "Let him that thinketh he standeth take heed lest he fall." If a Church lose the Spirit of God, there is no depth of corruption to which it may not rapidly descend; and a degraded Church is the most potent factor of national decay.

Allow me to say, in closing, that I believe the question, what is to be the type and the tone of the ministry in any generation, is decided in the theological seminaries. What the students are there, the ministers of the country will be by-and-by. And, while the discipline of the authorities and the exhortations and examples of professors may do something, the tone of the college is determined by the students themselves. The state of feeling in a theological seminary ought to be such, that any man living a life inconsistent with his future profession should feel thoroughly uncomfortable, and have the conviction driven in upon his conscience every day, that the ministry is no place for him.

VI.

THE PREACHER AS A MAN

LECTURE VI.

THE PREACHER AS A MAN.

IN the foregoing lectures I have finished, as far as time permitted, what I had to say on the work of our office, as it is illustrated by the example of the prophets; and to-day we turn to the other branch of the subject—to study the modern work of the ministry in the light cast upon it by the example of the apostles.

When we quit the Old Testament and open the New, we come upon another great line of preachers to whom we must look up as patterns. The voice of prophecy, after centuries of silence, was heard again in John the Baptist, and his ministry of repentance will always have its value as indicating a discipline by which the human spirit is prepared for comprehending and appreciating Christ. I have already given the reason why I am not at present to touch on the preaching of Christ Himself, although the subject draws one's mind like a magnet. After Christ, the

first great Christian preacher was St. Peter; and
between him and St. Paul there are many subordinate
figures, such as Stephen, Philip the Evangelist and
Apollos, beside whom it would be both pleasant and
profitable to linger. But we have agreed to take
St. Paul as the representative of apostolic preaching,
and I will do so more exclusively than I took Isaiah
as the representative of the prophets.

It is, I must confess, with regret that I pass
St. Peter by. There is a peculiar interest attaching
to him as the first great Christian preacher; and
there is something wonderfully attractive in his rude,
but vigorous and lovable personality. Besides, a
study of the influences by which he was transmuted
from the unstable and untrustworthy precipitancy
of his earlier career into the rocklike firmness which
made him fit to be a foundation-stone on which the
Church was built would have taught us some of the
most important truths which we require to learn;
because these influences were, first, his long and close
intimacy with Christ and, secondly, the outpouring
on him, at Pentecost, of the Holy Spirit; and there
are no influences more essential than these to the
formation of the ministerial character.

But I have no hesitation in devoting to St. Paul
the remainder of this course; because, as I indicated
in the opening lecture, there is no other figure in any

age which so deserves to be set up as the model of Christian ministers. In him all the sides of the ministerial character were developed in almost super-natural maturity and harmony; and, besides, the materials for a full delineation are available. It is my intention to speak of St. Paul, first, as a Man; secondly, as a Christian; thirdly, as an Apostle; and fourthly, as a Thinker.

To-day, then, we begin with St. Paul as a Man. If I had had time to set before you what St. Peter's life has to teach us, its great lesson would have been what Christianity can make of a nature without special gifts and culture, and how the two influences which formed him—intimacy with Christ and the outpouring of the Spirit—can supply the place of talents and educational advantages; for it is evident that, but for Christ, Peter would never have been anything more than an unknown fisherman. But St. Paul's case teaches rather the opposite lesson—how Christianity can consecrate and use the gifts of nature, and how talent and genius find their noblest exercise in the ministry of Christ. Paul would, in all probability, have made a notable figure in history, even if he had never become a Christian; and, although he himself delighted to refer all that he became and did to Christ, it is evident that the big nature of the man entered also as a factor into his Christian history.

Once at least St. Paul recognises this point of view himself, when he says, that God separated him to His service from his mother's womb. In Jeremiah's mind the same idea was awakened still more distinctly at the time of his call, when Jehovah said to him, " Before I formed thee in the belly I knew thee, and, before thou camest forth out of the womb, I sanctified thee, and I ordained thee a prophet unto the nations." This implies that, in the original formation of his body and mind, God conferred on him those gifts which made him capable of a great career. Here we touch on one of the deepest mysteries of existence. There is nothing more mysterious than the behaviour of Nature, when in her secret laboratories she presides over the shaping of the rudiments of life and distributes those gifts, which, according as they are bestowed with an affluent or a niggardly hand, go so far to determine the station and degree which each shall occupy in the subsequent competitions of the world. It is especially mysterious how into a soul here and there, as it passes forth, she breathes an extra whiff of the breath of life, and so confers on it the power of being and doing what others attempt to be and do in vain.

Undoubtedly St. Paul was one of these favourites

of fortune. Nature designed him in her largest and noblest mould, and hid in his composition a spark of celestial fire. This showed itself in a certain tension of purpose and flame of energy which marked his whole career. He was never one of those pulpy, shapeless beings who are always waiting on circumstances to determine their form; he was rather the stamp itself, which impressed its image and superscription on circumstances.

1. He was a supremely ethical nature. This perhaps was his fundamental peculiarity. Life could under no circumstances have seemed to him a trifle. The sense of responsibility was strong in him from the beginning. He was trained in a strict school; for the law of life prescribed to the race of which he was a member was a severe one; but he responded to it, and there never was a time when to receive the approval of God was not the deepest passion of his nature. Touching the righteousness which was in the law, he was blameless. After his conversion he laid bare unreservedly the sins of his past; but there were none of those dalliances with the flesh to confess into which soft and self-indulgent natures easily fall. He could never have allowed himself that which would have robbed him of his self-respect. His sense of honour was keen. When, in his subsequent life, he was accused of base things—lying, hypocrisy, avarice

and darker sins—he felt intense pain, crying out like one wounded, and he hurled the accusations from him with the energy of a self-respecting nature. It was always his endeavour to keep a conscience void of offence not only towards God, but also towards men; and one of his most frequently reiterated injunctions to those who were in any way witnesses for Christ was to seek to approve themselves as honest men even to those who were without. He was speaking out of his own heart when he said to all, "Whatsoever things are true, whatsoever things are honest, whatsoever things are pure, whatsoever things are lovely, whatsoever things are of good report: if there be any virtue, and if there be any praise, think on these things."

I cannot help pausing here to say, that he will never be a preacher who does not know how to get at the conscience; but how should he know who has not himself a keen sense of honour and an awful reverence for moral purity? We are making a great mistake about this. We are preaching to the fancy, to the imagination, to intellect, to feeling, to will; and, no doubt, all these must be preached to; but it is in the conscience that the battle is to be won or lost.* The great difficulty of missionary work is

* "The Sybarites of to-day will tolerate a sermon which is delicate enough to flatter their literary sensuality; but it is their taste which is

that in the heathen there is, as a rule, hardly any
conscience : it has almost to be created before they
can be Christianized. In many parts of Christendom
it is dying out ; and, where it is extinct, the whole
work of Christianity has to be done over again.

2. St. Paul's intellectual gifts are so universally
recognised that it is hardly worth while to refer to
them. They are most conspicuously displayed in his
exposition of Christianity, on which I shall speak in
the closing lecture. But in the meantime I remark,
that his intellectual make was not at all that usually
associated in our minds with the system-builder.

It was, indeed, massive, thorough and severe. But
it was not in the least degree stiff and pedantic. It
was, on the contrary, an intellect of marvellous flexi-
bility. There was no material to which it could not
adapt itself and no feat which it could not perform.
You may observe this, for example, in the diverse ways
in which he addresses different audiences. In one
town he has to address a congregation of Jews ; in
another a gathering of heathen rustics ; in a third
a crowd of philosophers. To the Jews he invariably
speaks, to begin with, about the heroes of their
national history ; to the ignorant heathen he talks

---

charmed, not their conscience which is awakened : their principle of
conduct escapes untouched. . . . Amusement, instruction, morals, are
distinct *genres.*"—AMIEL.

about the weather and the crops; and to the
Athenians he quotes their own poets and delivers
a high-strung oration; yet in every case he arrives
naturally at his own subject and preaches the gospel
to each audience in the language of its own familiar
ideas. Even outside of his own peculiar sphere altogether, St. Paul was equal to every occasion. During
his voyage to Rome, when the skill of the sailors was
baffled and the courage of the soldiers worn out by
the long-continued stress of weather, he alone remained
cheerful and clear-headed; he virtually became cap-
tain of the ship, and he saved the lives of his fellow-
passengers over and over again.

We think of the intellect of the system-builder as
cold. But there is never any coldness about St. Paul's
mind. On the contrary, it is always full of life and
all on fire. He can, indeed, reason closely and con-
tinuously; but, every now and then, his thought
bursts up through the argument like a flaming geyser
and falls in showers of sparks. Then the argument
resumes its even tenor again; but these outbursts are
the finest passages in St. Paul. In the same way
Shakespeare, I have observed, while moving habitually
on a high level of thought and music, will, every now
and then, pause and, spreading his wings, go soaring
and singing like a lark sheer up into the blue. When
the thought which has lifted him is exhausted, he

gracefully descends and resumes on the former level ;
but these flights are the finest passages in Shakespeare.

3. The intellectual superiority of St. Paul is universally acknowledged ; and to those who only know
him at a distance this is his outstanding peculiarity.
But the close student of his life and character knows,
that, great as he was in intellect, he was equally great
in heart, perhaps even greater.   One of the subtlest
students of his life, the late Adolphe Monod, of the
French Church, has fixed on this as the key to his
character.   He calls him the Man of Tears, and shows
with great persuasiveness that herein lay the secret
of his power.

It is certainly remarkable, when you begin to look
into the subject, how often we see St. Paul in the
emotional mood, and even in tears.   In his famous
address to the Ephesian elders he reminded them that
he had served the Lord among them with many tears,
and again, that he had not ceased to warn everyone
night and day with tears.   It is not what we should
have expected in a man of such intellectual power.
But this makes his tears all the more impressive.
When a weak, effeminate man weeps, he only makes
himself ridiculous ; but it is a different spectacle
when a man like St. Paul is seen weeping ; because
we know that the strong nature could not have been
bent except by a storm of feeling.

His affection for his converts is something extraordinary.   Some have believed that there is evidence
to prove that in youth his heart had suffered a terrible
bereavement.   It is supposed that he had been married,
but lost his wife early.   He never sought to replace
the loss, and he never spoke of it.   But the affection
of his great heart, long pent up, rushed forth into the
channel of his work.   His converts were to him in
place of wife and children.   His passion for them is
like a strong natural affection.   His epistles to them
are, in many places, as like as they can be to love-
letters.   Listen to the terms in which he addresses
them: "Ye are in our heart to die and live with you";
"I will very gladly spend and be spent for you, though,
the more abundantly I love you, the less I be loved";
"Therefore, my brethren, dearly beloved and longed
for, so stand fast in the Lord, my dearly beloved."

To his fellow-labourers in the Gospel especially, his
heart went out in unbounded affection.   The long
lists of greetings at the close of his epistles, in which
the characters and services of individuals are referred
to with such overflowing generosity and yet with such
fine discrimination, are unconscious monuments to the
largeness of his heart.   He could hardly mention a
fellow-worker without breaking forth into a glowing
panegyric : " Whether any do inquire of Titus, he is
my partner and fellow-helper concerning you ; or our

brethren be inquired of, they are the messengers of the churches and the glory of Christ."

There is no more conclusive proof of the depth and sincerity of St. Paul's heart than the affection which he inspired in others; for it is only the loving who are loved. None perhaps are more discriminating in this respect than young men. A hard or pedantic nature cannot win them. But St. Paul was constantly surrounded with troops of young men, who, attracted by his personality, were willing to follow him through fire and water or to go on his messages wherever he might send them. And that he could win mature minds in the same way is proved by the great scene at Miletus, already referred to, where the elders of Ephesus, at parting with him, " all wept sore, and fell on Paul's neck and kissed him, sorrowing most of all for the word which he said, that they should see his face no more."

The nature of St. Paul's work no doubt immensely developed this side of his character, but, before passing from the subject, it is worth remembering how the circumstances of his birth and upbringing were providentially fitted to broaden his sympathies, even before he became a Christian. He was not simply a Jew, but a Hebrew of the Hebrews; and he felt all the pride of a child of that race to which pertained the adoption and the glory and the covenant, and the giving of the law, and the service of God, and the promises. He could always put himself in touch at once with a Jewish audience by going back on associations which were as dear to himself as to them. Yet, although so thoroughly a Jew, he belonged by birth to a larger world. He was not born within the boundaries of Palestine, where his sympathies would have been cramped and his horizon narrowed, but in a Gentile city, famous for its beauty, its learning and its commerce ; and he was, besides, a freeborn citizen of Rome. We know from his own lips that he was proud of both distinctions ; and he thus acquired a cosmopolitan spirit and learned to think of himself as a man amongst men.

Nor ought we, perhaps, to omit here to recall the fact, that he learned in his youth the handicraft of tent-making. This brought him into close contact with common men, whose language he learned to speak and whose life he learned to know—acquirements which were to be of supreme utility in his subsequent career.

Gentlemen, it is generally agreed that a certain modicum of natural gifts is necessary for those who think of entering the ministry. Here is Luther's list of the qualifications of a minister : you will observe that most of them are gifts of nature : 1. He should be able to teach plainly and in order. 2. He should have a good head. 3. Good power of language. 4. A good voice. 5. A good memory. 6. He should know when to stop. 7. He should be sure of what he means to say. 8. And be ready to stake body and soul, goods and reputation, on its truth. 9. He should study diligently. 10. And suffer himself to be vexed and criticized by everyone.

The first consciousness of the possession of unusual powers is not unfrequently accompanied by an access of vanity and self-conceit. The young soul glories in the sense, probably vastly exaggerated, of its own pre-eminence and anticipates, on an unlimited scale, the triumphs of the future. But there is another way in which this discovery may act. The consciousness of unusual powers may be accompanied with a sense of unusual responsibility, the soul inquiring anxiously about the intention of the Giver of all gifts in conferring them. It was in this way that Jeremiah was affected by the information that special gifts had been conferred on him in the scene to which I have already referred in this lecture. He concluded at once that he had been blessed with exceptional talents in order that he might serve his God and his country with them. And surely in a gifted nature there could be no saner ambition than, if God permitted it, to devote its powers to the ministry of His Son.

There is no other profession which is so able to absorb and utilise talents of every description. This is manifest in regard to such talents as those mentioned by Luther—a good voice, a good memory, etc. But there is hardly a power or an attainment of any kind which a minister cannot use in his work. How philosophical power can serve him may be seen in the preaching of Dr. Chalmers, whose sermons were always cast in a philosophical mould. The philosophy was not very deep ; it was not too difficult for the common man ; but it gave the preaching a decided air of distinction. How scientific acquirements may be utilised is shown in the sermons of some of our foremost living preachers, who find an inexhaustible supply of illustrations in their scientific studies. Literary style may supply the feather to wing the arrow of truth to its mark. That poetic power may serve the preacher it is not necessary to prove on the spot where Ray Palmer wrote " My faith looks up to Thee." Business capacity is needed in church courts and in the management of a congregation. In some other professions men have to bury half their talents ; but in ours there is no talent which will not find appropriate and useful exercise.

We perhaps lay too much stress, however, on intellectual gifts and attainments. These are the only ones which are tested by our examinations in college ; yet there are moral qualities which are just as essential.

The polish given by education tells, no doubt ; but the size of the primordial mass of manhood tells still more. In a quaint book of Reminiscences recently published from the pen of a notable minister of last generation in the Highlands of Scotland, Mr. Sage of Resolis, there is a criticism recorded, which was passed by a parishioner on three successive ministers of a certain parish : " Our first minister," said he, " was a man, but he was not a minister ; our second was a minister, but he was not a man ; and the one we have at present is neither a man nor a minister."

There is no demand which people make more imperatively in our day than that their minister should be a man. It is not long since a minister was certain of being honoured simply because he belonged to the clerical profession and wore the clerical garb. People, as the saying was, respected his cloth. But ours is a democratic age, and that state of public feeling is passing away. There is no lack of respect, indeed, for ministers who are worthy of the name ; perhaps there is more of it than ever. But it is not given now to clerical pretensions, but only to proved merit. People do not now respect the cloth, unless they find a man inside it.

Perhaps the educational preparation through which

we pass at college is not too favourable to this kind of power. In the process of cutting and polishing the natural size of the diamond runs the risk of being reduced. When we are all passed through the same mill, we are apt to come out too much alike. A man ought to be himself. Your Emerson preached this doctrine with indefatigable eloquence. Perhaps he exaggerated it ; but it is a true doctrine ; and it is emphatically a doctrine for preachers. What an audience looks for, before everything else, in the texture of a sermon is the bloodstreak of experience ; and truth is doubly and trebly true when it comes from a man who speaks as if he had learned it by his own work and suffering.

It will generally be noticed in any man who makes a distinct mark as a preacher that there is in his composition some peculiarity of endowment or attainment on which he has learned to rely. It may be an emotional tenderness as in McCheyne, or a moral intensity as in Robertson of Brighton, or intellectual subtlety as in Candlish, or psychological insight as in Beecher. But something distinctive there must be, and, therefore, one of the wisest of rules is, Cultivate your strong side.

But what tells most of all is the personality as a whole. This is one of the prime elements in preaching. The effect of a sermon depends, first of all, on

what is said, and next, on how it is said ; but, hardly
less, on who says it. There are men, says Emerson,
who are heard to the ends of the earth though they
speak in a whisper.* We are so constituted that
what we hear depends very much for its effect on
how we are disposed towards him who speaks. The
regular hearers of a minister gradually form in their
minds, almost unawares, an image of what he is, into
which they put everything which they themselves
remember about him and everything which they have
heard of his record ; and, when he rises on Sunday in
the pulpit, it is not the man visible there at the moment
that they listen to, but this image, which stands
behind him and determines the precise weight and
effect of every sentence which he utters.

Closely connected with the force of personality is
the other power, which St. Paul possessed in so

* The finest description of a speaker known to me is this of Lord
Bacon in Ben Jonson's *Discoveries* ; and it is evident that it was the
man rather than the manner or even the matter which made the impression : "Yet there happened in my time one noble speaker, who
was full of gravity in his speaking. His language, where he could
spare or pass by a jest, was nobly censorious. No man ever spake
more neatly, more pressly, more weightily, or suffered less emptiness,
less idleness, in what he uttered. No member of his speech but consisted of his own graces. His hearers could not cough, or look aside
from him, without loss. He commanded where he spoke; and had
his judges angry and pleased at his devotion. No man had their
affections more in his power. The fear of every man that heard him
was, lest he should make an end."

supreme a degree, of taking an interest in others.   It
is the manhood in ourselves which enables us to
understand the human nature of our hearers ; and we
must have had experience of life, if we are to preach
to the life of men.

Some ministers do this extremely little.   Not once
but many a time, I have heard a minister on the
Sabbath morning, when he rose up and began to
pray, plunging at once into a theological meditation ;
and in all the prayers of the forenoon there would
scarcely be a single sentence making reference to the
life of the people during the week.   Had you been
a stranger alighted from another planet, you would
never have dreamed that the human beings assembled
there had been toiling, rejoicing and sorrowing for six
days ; that they had mercies to give thanks for and
sins to be forgiven; or that they had children at home
to pray for and sons across the sea.

There is an unearthly style of preaching, if I may
use the term, without the blood of human life in it :
the people with their burdens in the pews—the
burden of home, the burden of business, the burden
of the problems of the day—whilst, in the pulpit, the
minister is elaborating some nice point, which has
taken his fancy in the course of his studies, but has
no interest whatever for them.   Only now and then
a stray sentence may pull up their wandering atten

tion. Perhaps he is saying, " Now some of you may reply " ; and then follows an objection to what he has been stating which no actual human being would ever think of making. But he proceeds elaborately to demolish it, while the hearer, knowing it to be no objection of his, retires into his own interior.

If what was said in a former lecture about the distinctive difference between the preaching of the Old Testament and that of the New be considered, it will at once be recognised how vital is this aspect of the matter. The prophets of the Old Testament, in common with the thinkers of antiquity in general, thought of men in masses and regarded the individual only as a fragme nt of a larger whole. But Christ introduced an entirely new way of thinking. To Him the individual was a whole in himself; beneath the habiliments of even the humblest member of the human family there was hidden what was more precious than the entire material world ; and on the issues of every life was suspended an immortal des- tiny. This faith may be said to have made Jesus Christ the Saviour of the world ; for He saw in the lost children of men that which made Him live to seek them and die to save them. And it is by this same faith and vision that anyone is qualified to be a fellow-worker with Christ. No one will ever be able to engage with any success in the work of human

salvation who does not see men to be infinitely the
most interesting objects in the world, and who does
not stand in awe before the solemn destiny and the
sublime posssibilities of the soul. It is by the growth
and the glow of this faith that the worth of all
ministerial work is measured.

It is far easier, however, to acknowledge this view
in the abstract than to cherish it habitually towards
the actual men and women of our own sphere and
our own vicinity. That man is the most interesting
object in the world ; that the soul is precious ; and that
it is better for a human being to lose the whole world
than to miss his destiny—these are now common-
places, which everyone who bears the Christian name
will acknowledge. Yet in reality few live under their
power. Many a one who has paid the tribute of love
and admiration to the spectacle of Christ's compassion
for the outcasts, and melted with æsthetic emotion
before a picture of the Woman taken in Adultery
or the Woman that was a Sinner, has never once
attempted to save an actual woman of the same
kind in his own city, and would be utterly at a loss
if such a one, in an hour of remorse, were to throw
herself on his pity and protection. There is a great
difference between a sinner in a book or a picture
and a sinner in the flesh. Multitudes in their hearts
believe that all the remarkable and interesting people

lived long ago or that, at any rate, if any are now alive, they live many miles away from their vicinity. They believe that there were remarkable people in the first or the ninth century, but by no means in the nineteenth ; they believe that there are interesting people in Paris or London or New York ; but they have never discovered anything wonderful in those living in their own village or in their own street. Many who consider themselves enlightened will tell you that their neighbours are a poor lot. They fancy that, if they were living somewhere else, fifty or a hundred miles away, they would find company worthy of themselves ; though it is ten to one that, if they made the change, their new neighbours would be a poor lot also.

If a minister allows himself to harbour sentiments of this sort, he is lost.* No one will ever win men who does not believe in them. The true minister must be able to see in the meanest man and woman

---

* It has often astonished me to observe how easily ministers' wives in this respect find for themselves the right path. One would think it would be very difficult sometimes for those who have been brought up in cities or in a secluded circle to adapt themselves suddenly to a remote and unselect society ; and they have not, like their husbands, had the opportunity of meditating long on the duties of a public position. A hearty and cordial humanity in the members of a minister's family lends an immense assistance to his work. A minister ought to belong to no class of society, but to have the power of moving without constraint in every class.

a revelation of the whole of human nature ; and in the peasant in the field, and even the infant in the cradle, connections which reach forth high as heaven and far as eternity. All that is greatest in king or kaiser exists in the poorest of his subjects ; and the elements out of which the most delicate and even saintly womanhood is made exist in the commonest woman who walks the streets. The harp of human nature is there with all its strings complete ; and it will not refuse its music to him who has the courage to take it up and boldly strike the strings. The great preacher is he who, wherever he is speaking, among high or low, goes straight for those elements which are common to all men, and casts himself with confidence on men's intelligence and experience, believing that the just suggestions of reason and the terrors of conscience, the sense of the nobility of goodness and the pathos of love and pity are common to them all.*

Let me close this lecture with a few words on a great subject, to which a whole lecture might have been profitably devoted.

---

* "Not a heart but has its romance, not a life which does not hide a secret which is either its thorn or its spur. Everywhere grief, hope, comedy, tragedy ; even under the petrifaction of old age, as in the twisted forms of fossils, we may discover the agitations and tortures of youth. This thought is the magic wand of poets and preachers."— AMIEL.

No safer piece of advice could be tendered you than to let the beginning of your ministry be marked by care for the young. This is work which more than any other will encourage yourselves, and it is more likely than any other to establish you in the affections of a congregation.

To work successfully among children you must know their life and have the *entrée* of their little world of interests, excitements, prizes and hopes. It is not difficult to get it, if only we are simple and genuine. Children will approach their minister gladly and make him their confidant, if only he is accessible to them. By the ministers of an older generation they were kept at an awful distance. When they were out of temper or doing wrong, they were threatened with a visit from the minister in the same way as they might be threatened with the policeman, or the parish beadle, or a still more awful functionary of the universe. This, let us hope, has passed away, and in most parishes a ministerial visit is spoken of as a promise instead of a threat. A minister is proud nowadays if a child flies up to him in the street and ruffles his feathers with boisterous familiarity, or if a group of children pin him into the corner of a room and order him, under pains and penalties, to tell them a story. We are returning to the ideal of Goldsmith, in the *Deserted Village* :—

> " The service past, around the pious man
>   With steady zeal each loyal rustic ran ;
>   Even children followed with endearing wile,
>   And plucked his gown to share the good man's smile."

More important even than accessibility is genuine respect for the children.

We ought to respect their intelligence. When we are preaching to them, we should give them our very best. I venture to say, that a much larger proportion of the sermons preached to children is never written out than of sermons to adults. The preacher, having thought of two or three lines of remark and got hold of two or three stories, enters the pulpit with these materials lying loosely in his mind, and trusts to the moment for the style of the sermon. Of course, if a man has trained himself to preach in this way always, it is all right ; but, if not, it is a mistake. Children are greatly affected by felicity of arrangement and the music of language ; they do not know to what their pleasure is due, but they feel it ; and, if a preacher has the power of original thought or of beautiful diction, there is no occasion when he should be more liberal in the use of it than when he is addressing them.* The truth is, it is a complete

---

* This may be a reason for rather devoting a whole diet of worship to the children once a month or once a quarter than only giving them a few minutes every Sabbath. But many follow the latter practice with excellent results. Perhaps there ought to be something specially for

mistake to make the children's sermon so different
from other sermons as to create the impression that
it is the only utterance from the pulpit to which they
are expected to listen. It is not easy to get children
to begin to listen at all to what is said in church; the
children's sermon is a device to catch their attention;
but it ought also to be a bridge conducting them
over to the habit of listening to all that is said
there. If they acquire the habit, they are our best
hearers. A boy of twelve or thirteen can follow
nearly anything; and there is no keener critic of
the logic of a discourse or warmer appreciator of any
passage which is worthy of admiration.

But, while we respect the intelligence of the young,
there is something else which we need to believe in
still more. We do not half realise the drama of
religious impression going on in the minds of children.
We forget our own childhood and the movements
excited in our childish breasts under the preaching of
the Word—how real the things unseen were to us;
how near God was, His eye flashing on us through
the darkness; how our hearts melted at the sufferings
of Christ; how they swelled with unselfish aspirations

the children at every service. If I may mention my own practice, I
have, during my whole ministry, preached to children once a month;
and every Sunday I have a children's hymn in the forenoon and a
prayer for children in the afternoon.

as we listened to the stories of heroic lives ; how distinctly the voice of conscience spoke within us ; and
how we trembled at the prospect of death, judgment
and eternity.   What we were then, other children are
now ; and what went on in us is going on in them.
It is the man who believes this and reveres it who
will reap the harvest in the field of childhood.

There is no surer way to secure for ourselves the
interest of the old than to take an interest in the
young.   Of course a forced interest in children, shown
with this in view, would be hypocrisy and deserve
contempt.   We must love the children for their own
sakes.   Yet we may quite legitimately nourish our
interest in the young by observing that it is one of
the strongest instincts of human nature which makes
fathers and mothers feel kindnesses shown to their
children to be the greatest benefits which can be
conferred on themselves.   An Edinburgh minister,*
who has had conspicuous success in preaching to
children as well as in every other department of the
work of his sacred office, once, in a gathering of
divinity students, of whom I was one, told an incident
from his own life which is almost too sacred to be
repeated by any lips except his own, but which I
hope he will excuse me for enriching you with, as it

* Rev. J. H. Wilson, D.D.

puts in a memorable form one of the truest secrets of ministerial success. On the morning of the day when he was going to be ordained to his first charge, he was leaving his home in the country to travel to the city, and his mother came to the door to bid him good-bye. Holding his hand at parting, she said, "You are going to be ordained to-day, and you will be told your duty by those who know it far better than I do; but I wish you to remember one thing which perhaps they may not tell you—remember, that, whenever you lay your hand on a child's head you are laying it on its mother's heart."

VII.

THE PREACHER AS A CHRISTIAN

LECTURE VII.

THE PREACHER AS A CHRISTIAN.

IN last lecture I spoke of St. Paul as a Man, showing how remarkable were his endowments and
acquirements, and how these told in his apostolic
career. But it was not through these that he was
what he was. Great as were the gifts bestowed on
him by nature and cultivated by education, they were
utterly inadequate to produce a character and a
career like his. It was what Christianity added to
these that made him St. Paul.

It is right enough that we should now recognise
the importance of his natural gifts and trace out
the ways in which Providence was shaping his life
towards its true aim before he was conscious of it.
But St. Paul himself had hardly patience for such
cool reflections. He turned away with strong aver-
sion from his pre-Christian life as something condemned and lost ; and he delighted to attribute all
that he was and did to the influence of Christ alone.
In last lecture I quoted a single passage to show that

he himself recognised that his natural endowments had been bestowed in order to fit him for the peculiar work which he was destined to accomplish in the world ; but I question if from all his writings I could have quoted another passage to the same effect. It was only for a moment that he allowed himself to stand on this point of view ; whereas we could quote from every part of his writings such sayings as these : " By the grace of God I am what I am " ; " I laboured more abundantly than they all, yet not I, but the grace of God in me " ; " It is no more I that live, but Christ liveth in me."

That this was his habitual way of estimating his own achievements is strikingly illustrated by his mode of thinking and speaking of certain defects in the equipment with which nature had supplied him for the career on which he was embarked. Gifted as he was, even he did not possess all gifts. He lacked one or two of those which might have been thought most essential to his success.

It would appear that he lacked the rotund voice and copious diction of the orator ; for his critics were able to allege that, whilst his written style was powerful, his spoken style was contemptible. Painters have represented him as a kind of demi-god, with the stature of an athlete and the grace of an Apollo. But he seems to have been diminutive in stature ;

and there appears to be evidence to prove that there was that in his appearance which, at first sight, rather repelled than attracted an audience. He felt these defects keenly, and could not but wish sometimes that they were removed. But his habitual and settled feeling about them was, that he ought to look upon them as sources of strength rather than as weaknesses, because they made him rely the more on the strength of Christ. This was an unfailing resource, on which he felt that he could draw without limit. And so he gloried in his infirmities, that the power of Christ might rest upon him.*

It might be said that it was only the enthusiasm of Paul which made him attribute to Christ that which

---

* The most charming chapter of Adolphe Monod's *Saint Paul* is on the subject of these two paragraphs. It is difficult to quote from it, because one would like to quote it all; but I allow myself the pleasure of borrowing these golden sentences: " C'est qu'en dépit de tant de promesses faites à la foi, nous sommes toujours plus ou moins affaiblis par un reste de force propre, comme nous sommes toujours plus ou moins troublés par un reste de propre justice, que les plus humbles eux-mêmes traînent partout avec eux. Cette malheureuse force propre, cette éloquence propre, cette science propre, cette influence propre, forme en nous comme un petit sanctuaire favori, que notre orgueil jaloux tient fermé à la force de Dieu, pour s'y réserver un dernier refuge. Mais si nous pouvions devenir enfin faibles tout de bon et désespérer absolument de nous-mêmes, la force de Dieu, se répandant dans tout notre homme intérieur et s'infiltrant jusque dans ses plus secrets replis, nous remplirait jusqu'en toute plénitude de Dieu ; par où, la force de l'homme étant échangée contre la force de Dieu, rien ne nous serait impossible, parce que rien n'est impossible à Dieu."

really belonged to himself. But his own point of view is the just one. It was Christ who made him; and, if we are to understand a ministry like his, we must try to measure the influence of Christ upon him, or, in other words, investigate the elements of his Christianity.

1. Paul could claim that even in his pre-Christian days he had lived in all good conscience towards both God and man. Yet this profession of uprightness does not prevent him from confessing elsewhere that deep down in his consciousness there had been a mortal struggle between the principles of good and evil, in which the good was far from always winning the victory : "We all," he acknowledges, "had our conversation in times past in the lusts of our flesh, fulfilling the desires of the flesh and of the mind, and were by nature the children of wrath even as others." In the seventh chapter of Romans he has drawn a picture of this struggle, and it is to the very life. Theologians have, indeed, disputed among themselves as to the stage of experience there referred to— whether it is the state of an unconverted or of a converted man. But the human heart has no difficulty in interpreting it. The more thoroughly anyone is a man, the more easily will he understand it ; and especially the more upright and conscientious anyone is, the more certainly must he have experienced what

is described in words like these, " That which I do 1
allow not, for what I would that do I not, but what
I hate that do I " ; " For the good that I would I do
not, but the evil that I would not that I do " ; " I
find, then, a law that, when I would do good, evil is
present with me. For I delight in the law of God
after the inward man ; but I see another law in my
members warring against the law of my mind, and
bringing me into captivity to the law of sin which is
in my members. Oh wretched man that I am ! who
shall deliver me from the body of this death ? " Thus
Paul had been a lost man, in hopeless bondage to sin.

But he had to repent of his own righteousness as
well as of his sin. He had inherited the passionate
longing of the Jewish race for fellowship with God—
the longing expressed a hundred times in the poetry
of his fathers in words like these : " As the hart
panteth after the waterbrooks, so panteth my soul
after Thee, O God " ; " My soul thirsteth for God, for
the living God ; when shall I come and appear before
God ? " He had been taught that the great prize of
life is to be well-pleasing to God, and he had learned
the lesson with all the passionate earnestness of his
nature. Yet he never could attain to that for which
he longed. There always seemed to be a cloud on
the Divine face, and he was kept at a distance.
Luther went through the very same experience. His

was also a passionately religious nature, and he strove
with all his might to get into the sunshine of God's
face ; but his efforts were entirely baffled. Wash them
as he would, his hands were never clean.

What could an earnest nature do in such circumstances but seek to bring still greater sacrifices ?
Probably this was the source of Paul's zeal in the
work of the persecutor. He was vindicating the
honour of God when he exterminated the enemies of
God. The work must have gone sorely against the
grain of a nature as sensitive as his, especially when
he saw scenes, like the death of Stephen, in which the
gentleness and heroism of his victims shone out with
unearthly beauty. But he only flung himself more
passionately into his task ; because, the more trying
it was, the greater was the merit of doing it, and
the more certain was he of winning at last the full
approval of God.

This portion of Paul's career seems to be capable
of complete vindication on the ground of conscien-
tiousness. Indeed, in reviewing it, he stands sometimes on this point of view himself, and says that God
had mercy on him because he did it ignorantly in
unbelief. But oftener he thinks of it with overwhelming shame and remorse. The whole course of life
which had logically led up to work so inhuman in its
details and so directly in the face of God's purposes

was demonstrated by the issue to have been utterly ungodly. His thoughts had not been God's thoughts nor his ways God's ways. The scenes of the persecution, when, haling men and women, he cast them into prison ; the hatred and fury which in those days had raged in his breast ; the efforts which he had put forth to oppose the cause of Christ, which it was his firm resolution to extinguish to its last embers—these memories would never afterwards quit his mind. They kept him humble ; for he felt that he was the least of the apostles, who was not worthy to be called an apostle, because he had persecuted the Church of God. He called himself the chief of sinners, and believed that God had in his case exhaustively displayed the whole wealth of His mercy for a pattern to all subsequent generations.

The first element of St. Paul's Christianity, then, was the penitence of a lost man and a great sinner, who owed to Christ the forgiveness of his sins and the redemption of his life from an evil career. And he believed that Christ had purchased these benefits for him by the sacrifice of His own life.

2. The second great element of St. Paul's Christianity was his Conversion. This event fixed a gulf between the portion of his life which preceded it and that which followed. It formed the chief date of his life, and confronted him every time he looked back.

It influenced him in innumerable ways ; but its most signal effect, on which we shall do well to linger, was to set up Christ in his mind as a living Person, of whose existence he was absolutely assured.

Probably Paul's opposition to Christianity was from the first very specially opposition to Christ Himself. When he struck at the disciples, he was really striking at the Master through them. It is easy to conceive what an affront the pretensions of Jesus must have been felt to be by Paul. Jesus had been a man of about his own age—a young man ; he had sprung from the lowest of the people, being a villager and mechanic ; he had never sat in the schools of learning ; the men of ability and authority had had no hesitation in condemning Him. That such a one should be esteemed the Messiah of the Jews and worshipped as if He were Divine, raised a storm of indignation in the heart of Paul.

Probably nothing could have converted him except the miraculous occurrence which God employed. Christ had to come to him in person and in a visible shape—in the shape of the glorified humanity which He wears somewhere in that empire of God which we call heaven. Paul knew the light in which he was enveloped to be a Divine light ; the sound of the voice calling him was the thunder which from of old had been recognised by the race to which he belonged as the voice of God ; he was looking straight up to the place of God ; and in that place he saw Jesus, whom he was persecuting. Most Divine of all, however, were the sweetness, the clemency and the respect of the words in which he was addressed. This Jesus, against whom he was raging, came to him, not with corresponding rage, to take vengeance and destroy him, but with winning words of ruth and with the call to a high and blessed vocation. It was this which broke the heart of Paul and attached him to Christ for ever.

He always afterwards believed that what took place on this occasion was what I have said—that Jesus of Nazareth descended from the right hand of God to prove to him who He was and to claim him as His servant and apostle—and never afterwards did he for a moment doubt that the man whom his fellow-countrymen had crucified, and whom he himself had persecuted, was seated on the throne of heaven, clothed with Divine blessedness and omnipotence.

Of course others have doubted this. It may be said that what Paul saw was only a vision, and that therefore his new life was founded on a mistake. I believe his own account to be the correct one ; but perhaps we need not dogmatize too much about what he saw ; because it was not in reality on any theory of this vision that his faith was founded. It was not because he saw Christ that day with the bodily eye, or believed he did so, that he became or continued a Christian ; it was because, trusting Christ, thus revealed, he obtained that for which he had all his life been longing : he was no longer banished or kept at a distance, but brought nigh to God ; he was reconciled, and the love of God was shed abroad in his heart. He had all his lifetime been asking in despair, " What must I do to be saved? " but now he was saved. The humiliating bondage in which his spiritual nature had been held was dissolved, and, following Christ, he advanced from victory to victory.

This is the test of all conversions ; it is the best evidence of Christianity ; and it is the power of preaching. We believe in Christ not only because there is sufficient historical evidence that He existed eighteen hundred years ago and did such acts as proved that He was sent from God, but because He proves Himself to be living now by the transformation which He brings to pass in those who put their trust in Him. We are certain that there is a Saviour, because He has saved ourselves. I am happy to see that this evidence of our religion is at present coming again to the front. One of your younger scholars, Dr. Stearns of Bangor, Maine, has developed it, in a book just published, with great breadth of theological knowledge ; and a former Yale lecturer, Dr. Dale of Birmingham, has given a telling exposition of it at the same time.* This is the vital force of preaching. We are witnesses to Christ—not merely to a Christ who lived long ago and did wonders, but to a Christ who is alive now and is still doing moral miracles. And the virtue of any man's testimony lies in his being able to say that he has himself seen the Christ whom he preaches to others, and himself experienced the power which he recommends others to seek.

3. After his conversion the whole life of St. Paul was comprehended in one word ; and this word was Christ. There has often in modern times been a Christianity which has contained very little of Christ. Mr. Sage, of Resolis, one of whose quaint sayings I quoted in last lecture, has solemnly left it on record that, when he was a student at Aberdeen, the Professor of Divinity, who was also Principal of the University, in a three years' course of lectures on the principles of the Christian religion, never once mentioned the name of Christ ; and in those times sermons were perfectly common in which there was not the slightest allusion to the Saviour. In our day this is entirely changed. Yet we are also surrounded with a Christianity which is extremely vague. Almost

---

* Stearns, *The Evidence of Christian Experience ;* Dale, *The Living Christ and the Four Gospels.*

every sentiment in which there is anything devout or humane receives the name of Christian; and the question which many are asking is how little it is necessary for one who claims the Christian name to believe and profess. Even this question may, indeed, in some cases indicate a state of mind far from unpromising, which demands the utmost pastoral sympathy and skill; but, if we wish to know what Christianity is in its power, we must not live in this unhealthy region, but find a Christianity in which the distinctively Christian element is not a minimum but a maximum. Such was St. Paul's Christianity. Its most prominent peculiarity was that there was so much of Christ in it. He expressed this in the characteristic saying, " To me to live is Christ," which was only a Greek way of saying, To me life is Christ; and, from whatever side we look at his life, we see that this was true.

Christ had obtained, and He retained, an extensive hold on his emotional nature. St. Paul's was a large heart, and it was all Christ's. We are shy of speaking of our personal feeling towards the Saviour; and we probably feel pretty often that the conventional terms of affection for Him, which are made use of, for example, in the hymns of the Church, transcend our actual experience. St. Paul, on the contrary, has no hesitation in employing about Christ the language commonly used to describe the most absorbing passion, when love is filling life with a sweet delirium and making everything easy which has to be done for the sake of its object. St. Paul's achievements and self-denials were almost more than human ; but his own explanation of them was simple : " The love of Christ constraineth us." He had to forego the prizes which to other men make life worth living ; but what did he care ? " I count them but dung," he says, " that I may win Christ." If only he retained one thing, he was willing to let all others go : " Who shall separate us from the love of Christ ? Shall tribulation, or distress, or persecution, or famine, or nakedness, or peril, or sword ? Nay, in all these things we are more than conquerors through Him that loved us. For I am persuaded that neither death, nor life, nor angels, nor principalities, nor powers, nor things present, nor things to come, nor height, nor depth, nor any other creature, shall be able to separate us from the love of God, which is in Christ Jesus our Lord." These sound like the fervours of first love ; but they are the words of a man at the height of his powers. And in old age he was still the same : still to him Christ was the star of life, and the hope of being with Him had annihilated the terrors of death : " I am in a strait betwixt two, having a desire to depart, and to be with Christ ; which is far better."

13

But Christ was enthroned in St. Paul's intellect no less than in his heart. It was an intellect vast in its compass and restless in its movements; but all its movements circled round Christ, and its most powerful efforts were put forth to reach the full height of His glory. Everyone acquainted with his writings knows how full of Christ they are. What is technically called his Christology is both splendid and profound; but, indeed, his whole thinking is Christological; he saw the whole universe in Christ.

Perhaps, however, we see even more suggestively how his whole mind was occupied with this subject by observing the way in which the mere incidental mention of the name of Christ sends him off into the most sublime statements regarding Him. For example, when he is speaking to husbands about loving their wives, the thought strikes him that this love is like that of Christ to His people; and he breaks forth: " Husbands, love your wives, even as Christ also loved the Church, and gave Himself for it; that He might sanctify and cleanse it with the washing of water by the word, that He might present it to Himself a glorious Church, not having spot, or wrinkle, or any such thing." In like manner, happening to be recommending generosity, he thinks of the generosity of Christ, and away He breaks into an incomparable description of His descent from the throne of the

Highest to the death of the cross : " Let this mind be in you, which was also in Christ Jesus, who, being in the form of God, thought it not robbery to be equal with God," and so on; and, not content with following Him down, in accordance with the thought with which he started, he pursues the subject under the impulse of sheer love, following Him up to the highest heaven : " Wherefore God also hath highly exalted Him, and given Him a name which is above every name : that at the name of Jesus every knee should bow, of things in heaven, and things in earth, and things under the earth, and that every tongue should confess that Jesus Christ is Lord, to the glory of God the Father." When is it that the mind thus starts off into a subject at any chance hint or suggestion, pouring out the most astonishing ideas in the most felicitous language ? It is only when it is possessed with it, and when its ideas are so hot and molten, that they are ready to avail themselves of any outlet.

What may be called the inner or spiritual life of St. Paul may most of all be said to have been all Christ. His own theory of this innermost life is that it is a kind of living over again of the life of Christ : we die with Him to sin ; we are buried with Him in baptism ; as He rose, so we rise again to newness of life ; He ascended to sit on the throne of the Father, and we are seated with Him in heavenly places. He is the very soil in which this life grows, and the atmosphere which it breathes ; a Christian is " a man in Christ," and all the functions of his interior and even of his exterior life are performed in this element : he speaks in Christ, he marries in Christ, he dies in Christ, and in the resurrection he will rise in Christ.

This is what would be called the mysticism of St. Paul ; and doctrines resembling this have sometimes been associated in religion with fantastic speculation and unpractical dreaming. In St. Paul, however, mysticism had no such results. If there was any part of his life on which the influence of Christ was more conspicuous than another, it was the practical part. To him any pretended connection or intercourse with Christ in secret had no meaning unless its outcome was visible in a Christlike life—" If any man have not the spirit of Christ, he is none of His."

To his own person he applied this principle in the most rigorous manner. Christ, he is fond of saying, lives in him ; he almost speaks as if in his flesh the Son of God had experienced a second incarnation ; but he relentlessly draws the practical conclusion. When Christ lived in His own earthly tabernacle, what did He live for ? It was for the salvation of men ; He went about continually doing good ; He lived to seek and save the lost. If so, then, living in Paul, He must have the same purpose—to make use of his powers of mind and body for the salvation of the world. In this way Christ was really still carrying on the work which had been interrupted by His death. St. Paul dares to say that he is filling up that which was lacking of Christ's sufferings for the sake of His body, the Church. He says that the heart of Christ is yearning after men in his heart; that the mind of Christ is scheming for the kingdom of God in his brain; he even compares the marks of persecution on His body to the wounds of Christ.

There is nowhere else on record—at least there was not till St. Paul had taught it to the Christian world— such a merging of one life in another. And it is all the more remarkable when it is considered how big and strong a nature St. Paul's was. If any other man might have coveted an original and independent life, surely he was entitled to be something in the world; but he had utterly sunk himself into the echo and the organ of Another.*

---

* "I feel most strongly that man, in all that he does or can do which is beautiful, great or good, is but the organ and the vehicle of something or some one higher than himself. This feeling is religion. The religious man takes part with a tremor of sacred joy in those phenomena of which he is the intermediary but not the source, of which he is the scene but not the author, or rather the poet. He lends them voice, hand, will and help, but he is respectfully careful to efface himself, that he may alter as little as possible the higher work of the Genius who is making a momentary use of him. A pure emotion deprives him

Gentlemen, I have taken up nearly the whole of the lecture with this minute analysis of St. Paul's Christianity for two reasons.

I have done so, first, because I wish to create in your minds a genial estimate of the man himself whom I am setting up in this course of lectures as the model for preachers. It is not uncommon to speak as if the earliest apostles had been formed by their association with Jesus, and, strong only in their affection for Him, had gone forth to tell the world the simple story of His life and death ; but St. Paul, being a man of a colder nature and of strong intellectual proclivities, drew Christianity away from the person of Jesus and transmuted it into a hard intellectual system. I think I have proved that this is a totally mistaken impression, which does gross injustice to the great Apostle. None of the apostles, not even St. John, was more filled with the glow of personal attachment to Christ. He had a larger nature than any of them, but it was penetrated with this passion through and through. Being of the

of personality and annihilates the self in him. Self must perforce disappear when it is the Holy Spirit who speaks, when it is God who acts. This is the mood in which the prophet hears the call, the young mother feels the movement of the child within, the preacher watches the tears of his audience. So long as we are conscious of self, we are limited, selfish, held in bondage."—AMIEL.

intellectual type, he could not help thinking out Christianity : but Christ entered into every thought he had about it.

The other reason why I have attempted to analyze so fully to-day the Christian experience of Paul is because I believe that the great motive of the ministry lies here—the very pulse of the machine.*

There are many motives which may go to constitute a powerful ministry and enable us to rejoice in our vocation. I have dealt with some of them already in this course of lectures. There is, for example, the one which I mentioned in last lecture, that the ministry gives satisfying and exhilarating employment to all the powers of the mind. There is, again, that with which I dealt in an earlier lecture, that ours is a patriotic service : we are doing the very best for our country when we are permeating its life with the spirit of true religion. An aspect of the ministry which attracts many minds at present is that it is a service to humanity ; the heart and conscience of the age are stirred by the misery of the poor, and this is the most obvious and effective mode of rescue.

---

* As enthusiasm for Christ is the soul of preaching as far as the preacher is concerned, so in a spiritual congregation there will always be found a jealous desire for this element in what they hear.

These are inspiring motives; and others might be mentioned. But far more important than them all is a strong personal attachment to the Saviour. This is the motive of the ministry which goes deepest and wears longest.

It may have many roots. It may be rooted in impressive convictions about the person of the Saviour and enthusiastic admiration of His character. It may spring from a profound sense of the lost condition from which He has rescued ourselves and of the destiny to which He has raised us. It may be due most of all to the impression made on our mind and heart by the sacrifice at the cost of which Jesus procured salvation for us. And here the depth or shallowness of our theology will be sure to tell. If our views are superficial either of the difference which salvation has made to ourselves or of what Christ did to constitute Himself the Saviour, the likelihood is that we shall love little. It is the man who knows that he has been forgiven much and saved at a great cost, who loves much. And the amount of love is the measure of sacrifice.

In all ages this has been the secret of devoted lives. It has made the great preachers—St. Augustine and St. Bernard, Luther and Wesley, Samuel Rutherford and McCheyne. It has made those too who have not been great in the eyes of men, but by their self-denying lives have made the kingdom of God to come. In one of his sonnets Matthew Arnold tells of meeting with a minister, " ill and o'erworked," on a broiling August day in the East End of London, and asking him how he fared in that scene of sin and sorrow. " Bravely," was the answer, " for I of late have been much cheered with thought of Christ." It is said to have been an actual incident.* At all events, it is the explanation of thousands of heroic lives passed in similar desperate situations. At present the adherents of a humanitarian philanthropism are loud in proclaiming the woes of the world, as if they had been the first to discover them, and propounding schemes for their amelioration ; but their methods have all been anticipated by the humble followers of Jesus ; and nine-tenths of the genuine philanthropic work of the world are being done by men and women who make no noise, but who cannot help working for the ends of Jesus, because His love is burning in their very bones, and because the life of Christ in them cannot help manifesting itself after its kind. Down the Christian centuries there has come floating a kind of hymn : the words are said to be by St. Patrick : the sentiment may well be called the

---

* See an article by the Rev. John Kennedy, D.D., in *The Evangelical Magazine*, April 1891.

music to which the true Church militant has always
marched :—

> Christ with me, Christ before me,
> Christ behind me, Christ within me,
> Christ beneath me, Christ above me,
> Christ at my right, Christ at my left,
> Christ in the fort,
> Christ in the chariot seat,
> Christ in the poop,
> Christ in the heart of every man who thinks of me,
> Christ in the mouth of every man who speaks to me,
> Christ in every eye that sees me,
> Christ in every ear that hears me.

POSTSCRIPT.—Here may be introduced a few notes
which are to me of inestimable value.   The happiness
of my visit to the States, which was great, was over-
shadowed at the close by the news of the death of
the best friend I had on earth—the Rev. Robert W.
Barbour, of Bonskeid.   None who knew him will need
to have it explained why I should think of him at
this point ; because, while he had drunk deeply of the
spirit of the time and was possessed of a rare love for
men, the deepest source of the sacred extravagance
with which he lavished himself and his many talents
on every good cause was nothing else than the passion for Christ which I have tried in this lecture to
illustrate.   He took a warm interest in this course

of lectures, and sent me the following Aphorisms on Preaching, to be used as I might think fit. I re-produce them entire, as they came from him. Per-haps they were the very last literary work he did :—

The Book and the Library. The preacher must be master of many books, but servant of one.

Closet and Desk. Study as though thou mightest preach for fifty years ; pray as though thou mightest preach for five.

Divine and Human. Speak as though the mouth were God's ; but let the voice be a man's.

First and Second Aims. All gifts (presence, voice, gesture, culture, style, and so on) may be wings, if kept behind one's back ; the moment they are seen they become dead weights.

Two strings to one's bow will do with any shafts but the arrows of the King. Letters, the press, the lyre, the porch, must stand in the background behind " this one thing."

Think less and less of everything else ; and more and more of thy message.

Aims and No Aims. Aim at something, you will hit it ; also draw your bow at a venture.

" *Make full proof of thy ministry.*" Try every method—writing, reading, committing, extending, extemporising. Imitate every man, but mimic none. Nothing makes a preacher like preaching.

ᵧ *Pulpit Form.* Respect your hearers. Do not gird at them; angle for them—and agonize. Address yourself to one at a time—first to the man in the pulpit. He who has hit himself first will not miss others. He who trembles at the word of the Lord, men will tremble at his word. (Borrowed) A preacher must either be afraid of his audience or his audience of him.

Janua Domini. Always enter the pulpit by the Door (John x. 7).

Contents and Omissions. Put everything you can into every address. Omit everything you can from every address.

"*Faith cometh by hearing.*" Therefore, to begin with, be audible. The Sermon on the Mount commences thus: "He opened His mouth" (Matt. v. 2).

Time and Eternity. Speak to men's fleeting hopes and passing interests; speak also to their grey hairs and to their midnight hours.

Ultimata. Desire to prophesy (1 Cor. xiv. 1); covet to prophesy (*ib.* 39); do not preach if thou darest be silent. (1 Cor. ix. 16.)

LECTURE VIII.

THE PREACHER AS AN APOSTLE

LECTURE VIII.

THE PREACHER AS AN APOSTLE.

GENTLEMEN, in the two last lectures we have investigated two of the principal sources—perhaps I might say the two principal sources—of a minister's power—his manhood and his Christianity. These may be called the two natural springs out of which work for men and God proceeds. Out of these it comes as a direct necessity of nature. If any one is much of a man—if there be in him much fire and force, much energy of conviction—it will be impossible for him to pass through so great an experience as the reception of Christianity without making it known; and, if he be much of a Christian—if there be in him much of the spirit of Christ, which is the spirit of self-sacrifice and benevolence—it will be impossible for him to refrain from approaching men in their sin and misery and endeavouring to communicate to them the secret of blessedness. He will make but a poor minister who would not be an earnest worker for God and man, even if he were not a minister.

These impulses were conspicuously strong in St. Paul. Yet there was also another source from which he drew the motives of his ministry. This was the fact that God had appointed him to the office of an apostle and allotted him a specific sphere of activity as the apostle of the Gentiles.

The other two sources of motive are, as I have said, natural; this one, on the contrary, is official. This may raise a prejudice against it. So many and such grave mistakes have been made through regarding official appointment as the only warrant for Christian work, to the prejudice of the antecedent qualifications of a genuine and sympathetic manhood and a deep personal Christianity, without which it is nothing, that there is a disposition to ignore this kind of motive altogether. But St. Paul acknowledges it. Although he was always, no doubt, far more of a man and a Christian than an official, yet, in reply to opposition, he insists with great vehemence on his apostolic rank; and evidently he felt that this imposed on him additional obligations to be earnest and faithful in the work to which his manly and Christian instincts prompted him.

It is, indeed, of great consequence to any one who

has become a Christian, and who begins to feel stirring in his breast those impulses to serve God and bless the world which are native to the Christian spirit, to obtain a definite sphere to fill and a definite work to do. Otherwise these God-inspired impulses expressing themselves in mere words and sentiments gradually decay through want of exercise, or they are dispersed over so many objects that nothing is done. But, when a special task is obtained, the force of these sentiments is concentrated upon it and transmuted into actual work. The Christian man says : Here is my own task ; if I do not accomplish it, no one else can ; this is my corner in the great labour-field, which I, and no one else, have to make fruitful and beautiful ; I shall be answerable to the Judge of all at the last for the manner in which the work assigned to me is done.

Such sentiments had a strong hold of the mind of St. Paul. One of his commonest ways of thinking of his office was as a stewardship, which he was administering, and for which by-and-by he would have to render a reckoning. " And," says he, " it is required in stewards that a man be found faithful."*

---

* An indication of the intensity with which St. Paul's mind worked upon the subject of the ministry is to be found in the number and variety of his metaphors for it. The following are those which I

Similarly, he thought of himself as a workman with a certain portion of a temple to build; but the great Taskmaster was coming round in the evening to inspect the work—ay, and even to test it with fire; and, when that testing-time came, he desired to be a workman not needing to be ashamed. All the work of his apostleship appeared to him a curriculum which he had to cover before he could win the prize of the Divine approval. This is his favourite figure of speech, and he applies it in many directions.

For example, the athlete in the racecourse has to keep himself in training and to put every muscle on the stretch. So St. Paul felt the obligation to put every power he possessed into his work. "Give thyself wholly to them," he says to a young fellow-labourer about his duties; and what he preached he practised. "Stir up the grace of God that is in thee," he says to the same friend again; and he called on his own nature continually for the utmost exertion of its powers. He was always growing; but

---

have noted, but there may be more—nurse (1 Thess. ii. 7), father (1 Cor. iv. 15), gardener (1 Cor. iii. 6), labourer (1 Cor. iii. 9), builder (1 Cor. iii. 10), servant (1 Cor. iv. 1), bondman (2 Tim. ii. 24), steward (1 Cor. iv. 1), ambassador (Eph. vi. 20), soldier (1 Tim. vi. 12), herald (1 Tim. ii. 7), shepherd (Acts xx. 28), workman (2 Tim. ii. 15), athlete (1 Tim. iv. 7), vessel (2 Tim. i. 21).

the increment of his faculty and influence went all to the same object.

An athlete in the games naturally laid aside every weight, divesting himself of everything which might impede his running and rob him of the prize. He dared not glance aside at any object which would take his eye off the goal. So St. Paul sacrificed everything for the Gospel's sake ; he had but one end and no by-ends. He was often, indeed, accused of aiming at some end of his own. With especial persistency he was accused of avarice. It is very ludicrous now to think of this great man having been supposed capable of so mean a vice. But his motives were too high and pure to be intelligible to his accusers, and they naturally attributed to him the motive which was the strongest of which they were conscious themselves. But they only brought out the true greatness of the man. He believed in the right of preachers of the Gospel to live by the Gospel, and he looked forward to the general recognition of this as soon as Christianity had obtained a footing in the world. But he himself lived above all such claims. He accepted support from his converts, indeed, and thanked God for it, when he had good reason to think that his motives were understood. But, where they were suspected or the success of the Gospel seemed to be in any degree endangered by his acceptance of money, he would not take a cent, but would rather sit up half the night and work his fingers to the bone to earn his livelihood.   There is no sublimer scene in history than the great Apostle, who was bearing the weight of Christianity on his shoulders and carrying the future of the world beneath his robe, toiling with his hands for his living by the side of Aquila and Priscilla, in order that he might keep Christianity from being tarnished with the faintest suspicion of mercenary motives.

Gentlemen, among the many attractions of our calling on which I should like to congratulate you this is not the least, that it provides a definite sphere for the exercise of the benevolent impulses which you may feel as men and as Christians and, by exercising, develops them.   These impulses may be the strongest and most sacred in our nature.   But in other occupations, in the excitement and competition of life, they are in great danger of being slowly extinguished. In our calling, on the contrary, they receive constant opportunities of nurture and development.   Their healthy and spontaneous activity is the soul of ministerial work ; and this is stimulated by the sense of responsibility to fill the sphere allotted to us and exhaust its possibilities.

But, besides the sense of duty, there is a stimulus of a still more affecting kind which comes to a man when he is set over a congregation of his own.   When

I first was settled in a church, I discovered a thing of which nobody had told me and which I had not anticipated, but which proved a tremendous aid in doing the work of the ministry. I fell in love with my congregation. I do not know how otherwise to express it. It was as genuine a blossom of the heart as any which I have ever experienced. It made it easy to do anything for my people ; it made it a perfect joy to look them in the face on Sunday morning. I do not know if this is a universal experience ; but I should think it is common. For my part, I like to meet a man who thinks his own congregation, however small it may be, the most important one in the Church and is rather inclined to bore you with its details. When a man thus falls in love with his people, the probability is that something of the same kind happens to them likewise. Just as a wife prefers her own husband to every other man, though surely she does not necessarily suppose him to be the most brilliant specimen in existence, so a congregation will generally be found to prefer their own minister, if he is a genuine man, to every other, although surely not always entertaining the hallucination that he is a paragon of ability. Thus to love and to be loved is the secret of a happy and successful ministry.

Taking up the responsibilities of his office in the

spirit which I have described, St. Paul would have found any sphere, however limited, laborious. But, in point of fact, the sphere allotted to him was an enormous one. It was nothing less than the whole Gentile world.

The known world was not, indeed, in that age, of anything like the same dimensions as it is today. It consisted only of a narrow disc of countries round the shores of the Mediterranean. Yet to any other man the vocation to evangelize it all must have been bewildering and even paralyzing. St. Paul, however, accepted it in all seriousness, and ever afterwards, till the day of his death, he regarded the populations of these countries as people to whom he owed the message of the Gospel. Speaking of the two recognised divisions of the Gentile world of that day, he says, " I am debtor both to the Greeks and to the barbarians, both to the wise and to the unwise."

Of course he did not live long enough to preach the Gospel to all the inhabitants of even the little world of his day. Yet it is amazing to think of the range of his labours. He preached in nearly all the great cities of that world—in Antioch, Ephesus, Corinth, Athens, Rome and many others—his predilection for cities being obviously due to the hope that, when Christ was made known in these crowded centres, the sound of his doctrine would echo through the surrounding regions. And this hope was justified. The cities in the province of Asia, for example, to which St. John sent the letters in the beginning of Revelation, were probably all evangelized from Ephesus by converts of St. Paul, though he himself may have visited none of them but Ephesus. The passion burned continually in his mind to get forward and cover new ground. He could not bear to build on another man's foundation. The wide, unfulfilled provinces of his apostolate ever called him on.

His first journey was merely a circuit of the countries bordering to the west and north on his own native Cilicia, and lay chiefly among barbarians. But the second, after a still more extended tour among the barbarians, brought him to the borders of that wonderful world of culture and renown in which dwelt the Greeks as distinguished from the barbarians. He was standing on the shore of Asia and looking across to the shore of Europe. In Europe were the two great eyes of the Gentile world—Athens and Rome—the one the centre of its wisdom and the other of its power. How could the Apostle of the Gentiles help wishing to preach the Gospel there? He crossed the narrow strait, and then advanced from one Greek town to another, till he stood on the very spot where Socrates had taught and Demosthenes thundered. In his third journey he had to concentrate his work on

Ephesus; because, like a skilful general, he would not leave territory in the rear unconquered. But Rome was now the aim of all his desires—Rome, the very citadel of the world which he had to conquer. He approached it at last in the garb of a prisoner and in a gang of prisoners. But, as we follow him, we feel as if we were going with a victorious army to take part in a grand triumph. Indeed, as you accompany this great spirit, this is often the feeling you have. He had it himself. " Thanks be unto God," he says, "who always causeth us to triumph." Only to his mind the occupant of the car of victory was not himself, but Christ; he was only a satellite, showering largess in the name of the Victor among the crowd around the chariot-wheels.

Such is the image of the Apostle which grows on the imagination as we read his extraordinary life. Yet there was another side. To us now his career is heroic and glorious; but to him, at the time, it was beset with innumerable obstacles; and, wonderful as were his labours, more wonderful still were his sufferings. He went from town to town incessantly; but seldom did he leave any place without having been in peril of his life. Sometimes the mob rose against him and only left him when they had cast out of their town his apparently lifeless body, as they would have flung away the carcase of a dog. Sometimes the authorities apprehended him and subjected him to the rigour of the law. But hear the catalogue of his sufferings from his own lips : " Are they ministers of Christ ? I am more : in labours more abundant, in stripes above measure, in prisons more frequent, in deaths oft : of the Jews five times received I forty stripes save one, thrice was I beaten with rods, once was I stoned, thrice I suffered shipwreck, a night and a day I have been in the deep ; in journeyings often, in perils of waters, in perils of robbers, in perils by mine own countrymen, in perils by the heathen, in perils in the city, in perils in the wilderness, in perils in the sea, in perils among false brethren ; in weariness and painfulness, in watchings often, in cold and nakedness ; besides those things which are without, that which cometh upon me daily, the care of all the churches." Yet, when he wrote this, he was only midway in his career.

These incidents are glorified now by the influence of time, but, when they had to be endured, they were real and painful enough. To take but a single instance, what must it have been to a man of such sensitive honour and engaged only in doing good to be so frequently in the hands of the police and in the company of malefactors ? In his epistles he cannot conceal the irritation caused by his " chain." Although in victorious moods he felt himself, as we have seen, borne onwards in triumph, in other moods he felt himself at the opposite extreme: "I think that God hath set forth us the apostles last, as it were appointed to death ; for we are made a spectacle unto the world and to angels and to men ; we are made as the filth of the world, and are the offscourings of all things"; the reference being to the gladiators whose cheap lives were sacrificed to embellish the conqueror's triumph.

Yet it was never long before he could rally from such depression at the thought of the cause in which he suffered all ; and his habitual mood, in the face of accumulating difficulties, was expressed in these heart-stirring words : "None of these things move me, neither count I my life dear unto myself, so that I might finish my course with joy and the ministry which I have received of the Lord Jesus, to testify the Gospel of the grace of God."

It is good to linger beside one who was so faithful to his charge, so hard a worker and so patient a sufferer. We may learn from these extraordinary labours and sufferings to do honest work and to endure hardness ourselves.

Our sphere is, indeed, very different from his. His was so vast as to be almost limitless ; ours' may be very circumscribed. He was continually moving from place to place and encountering new people ;

we may have to labour among the same handful of people for a lifetime. He lived amidst daily novelty and excitement; we may have to fulfil an existence of deep monotony. And all the disadvantages do not belong to the large, difficult and dangerous lot. It may seem easy to be faithful in a small sphere and to exhaust all its possibilities. But the narrow lot has its trials as well as the wide one, and perhaps it does not require less virtue to overcome them. A stronger sense of duty may be needed to prepare an honest sermon week by week to a small and comparatively ignorant congregation than to bear the brunt of danger in an exposed post of the mission field.*

Nowhere can the ministry be easy if its responsibilities are realised and its duties honestly discharged. Look forward, I would say to you, to a laborious life. If you are thinking of the ministry otherwise, you had better turn back. Ours is a more crowded existence than that of any other profession.

---

* "Go where you can do most *for* men, not where you can get most *from* men.

Be more concerned about your ability than about your opportunity, and about your walk with God than either.

Your sphere is where you are most needed.

There is no place without its difficulties : by removing you may change them, it may be you will increase them ; but you cannot escape them."—PREDIGER.

There is the work of study and preaching. I do not know the details of a minister's week among you; but in Scotland ministers have, as a rule, two discourses to prepare for Sunday, besides a lesson for the Bible Class, which may involve as much work as a sermon; and we have at least one week-day meeting at which a lengthy address is given. For these four discourses subjects have to be found; materials for exposition and illustration have to be collected; the mind has first to make each subject its own and then to shape it into a form suitable for popular effect. A sermon may sometimes, indeed, come in a flash, and perhaps there is something of sudden discovery in the very best work; but even then, time is required to work out the thought and enrich it with subsidiary thinking; and there are many discourses which are of **no** value without extensive investigation and the patient working-up of the quarried materials. Then follows the writing. This will take at least six or eight hours for a discourse, and may easily take much more. Many ministers do not write more than one discourse a week fully out, and probably they are wise; but many write two. Here, then, there is obviously ample work for a long forenoon on five days of the week. I have always had to add the afternoon of Friday and Saturday, and often the evening as well. Then comes the hard and exciting work of Sunday. It is a religious duty to rest on Monday, as we do not get the bodily rest of the Sabbath.*

There is the work of visitation. The sick and the bed-ridden must be visited; and it is of enormous profit to visit the whole congregation from house to house. As Dr. Chalmers said, the directest way to a man's heart is generally through the door of his home. Acquaintance with the actual circumstances of the families of the congregation gives wonderful reality and point to the prelections of Sunday. Our sermons must rise out of the congregation if they are ever to reach down to it again. Here, it is evident, there is abundant work for the afternoons which study leaves free. Many ministers have to add one or two evenings, the evening being the best time to find their people at home.

There is a third mass of work of an exceedingly miscellaneous character which absorbs much time and strength. It includes such duties as performing the ceremonies at baptisms, marriages and funerals; organising the work of the congregation; attending church courts and sitting on committees; serving on school boards and the boards of benevolent

---

* "A sermon which costs little is worth as much as it has cost. Yet measure not the value of the sermon by the length and hardness of your labour."—DUPANLOUP.

societies; preaching from home and addressing the meetings of neighbour ministers; writing official letters; raising money; receiving visitors; writing for the press. It would be easy for ministers in positions of any prominence to spend their whole time in duties of this description, none of which might appear useless; so great is the multitude of the claims which pour in from every side.

I have said nothing of the time required for keeping abreast of the literature of the day or for cultivating an intellectual specialty. It is extraordinary what some of the busiest men achieve in this respect; but it is only managed by an economy and even penury of time for which a kind of genius is requisite. Of course there are seasons of the year when the pressure of public engagements is not so great; and ministers are allowed longer holidays than other professional men. A couple of hours a day given from a holiday to great reading may shoot threads of fresh colour through the whole web of a season's work. Nor have I said anything of the time necessary for thinking over the devotional portion of the service of the sanctuary, though in our churches, where free prayer prevails, this deserves as careful attention as the sermon.

This glimpse which I have given you into the details of a minister's week will help you to realise that the life which lies before you is a laborious one. Of course the labour may be shirked. Ministers have their time in their own hands; they have no office hours; and, I suppose, a minister's life may be more ignobly idle than any other professional man's. That is, if he has no conscience.

How far a man who is conscientious and works hard may be justified in devoting himself to one branch of ministerial work for which he has special aptitudes or predilections, it is difficult to judge. Perhaps the Protestant Church has failed in making use of special gifts. Some eminent preachers, for example, neglect pastoral visitation; * and there are, I suppose, many ministers who keep out of more general public work, because they have no taste for it. There may be some gain in this; but there is also loss. When a preacher does not visit, he is apt to become an orator, who dazzles but does not feed the flock. When a minister keeps himself apart from

---

* The first Sunday I was in America, I worshipped in the churches of Rev. Dr. W. M. Taylor and Rev. Dr. John Hall, who are, I suppose, the two most eminent ministers of New York; and I was astonished to hear both of them intimate that they would visit in certain streets during the week. There are no ministers anywhere more immersed than these in every kind of public duty; yet they find time for regular pastoral visitation. On coming home, I mentioned this fact to an equally eminent minister in this country. " Well," said he, " when I came to the city, the elders of my congregation advised me not to visit, and I followed their advice; but it was the worst advice I ever got."

public interests, the Church to which he belongs is likely to be weak at that point.

The most fatal neglect is that of study; and perhaps it is the commonest. The part of our work which needs most moral resolution is undoubtedly the sermon —to get it begun, studied, written and finished. It requires the discipline of years in even the most conscientious to win the mastery of themselves in this particular; and it is probably at this point that three-fourths of all ministerial failures take place. It is not the reading of the material bearing on the subject which is difficult; indeed, this may be luxuriously prolonged, till it is too late to think and write the sermon out. The hard and sour toil lies in facing the sweat of thought and the irksomeness of writing; although, when the difficulty is overcome, the happiness and triumph of our calling lie here also.

Of course this difficulty is greatest in the small sphere. Here the temptation is, to be overcome by the monotony of the situation, to allow the powers to stagnate, to feel that anything will do, and put the people off with that which has cost no exertion. " I know," says one who wields a trenchant pen,* " how plausible the excuses are, and I know what relaxation of study results in—laziness in the morning, increasing

---

* Dr. Marcus Dods.

excesses in the daily papers, increased interest in gardening, several more pipes a day, and so forth. Breakfast comes finally to its long-deferred end about ten ; then there is a consultation with the gardener, which is, of course, business, and makes the idler feel that really his active habits are returning ; then two letters have to be answered ; then, just as he means to go to his study, he sees Mr. Fritterday passing, and before he has finished his colloquy over the hedge with him, it is past midday. When he does get to his study, *Macmillan* or *Blackwood* is lying on his table, and he feels he cannot settle till he knows what is the fate of the heroine of the current story, or his window overlooks the busy hayfield of his neighbour, and he becomes ten times more interested in that work than in his own ; and so his whole forenoon is gone, and he is summoned to dinner before he has earned his salt by one decent hand's turn."

This kind of temptation, however, is not confined to the man in the small and easy situation : it is the common temptation of all ministers. Only in the city it comes in another form. The man who has a large congregation and a little popularity is beset with calls from every quarter to engage in every kind of duty outside his own sphere His doorbell never ceases ringing. Every applicant supposes his own

15

case the most important. There is a whirl of excitement, and there is an exhilaration in being able in many ways to serve the public. But, if the man gives up his habits of study, he is lost. His appearances become commonplace ; the public tire of him, and throw him aside as ruthlessly as they have senselessly idolised him. Robert Hall used to say that, when the devil saw that a minister was likely to be useful in the church, his way of disposing of him was to get on his back and ride him to death with engagements.

To follow the course of St. Paul's labours and sufferings on the grand scale produces an overwhelming impression of earnestness and devotion ; yet it is even more by entering into the minute details of his activity that we find the Apostle. One who has to deal with vast masses is apt to overlook details ; and it is so even in the work of Christ. An evangelist, for example, moving from place to place and surrounded with multitudes, may know very little of individuals. The minister of a large congregation is exposed to the same temptation. Indeed, we are all too desirous of crowds and too little occupied with the units of which they are composed. But this is the greatest of all mistakes. St. Paul, amidst the constant change of scene and the pressure of large bodies of

people in which he lived, never overlooked individuals
In his speech to the elders of Ephesus he could
challenge them to bear witness that he had taught
not only publicly but from house to house, and had
warned every one night and day with tears. While,
like his Master, he was moved by the sight of a multitude and welcomed the opportunity of making known
the glad tidings to many, he was quite as ready to
preach to the small company of women of whom
Lydia was one at the riverside or to the soldier to
whom he was chained in the Roman prison.

St. Paul was never a mere evangelist. The evangelist's work is to deal with the initial stage of the
Christian life : he has to bring men to decision ; and,
when this is done, he passes on, leaving to other
agencies whatever more may be required. An evangelist sometimes knows very little of what becomes of
his converts after he has quitted the place. But St.
Paul was as eager about this as about the first impressions. However small the company of the converted
might be, he formed them into a Christian Church,
and ordained elders in every city. He often left an
assistant behind to carry on and consolidate the work
which he had begun. When at a distance, he was
always eager for news about his churches. His epistles
are full of such anxieties ; and, indeed, his epistles
themselves are the best monument of his pastoral

care ; for they were written to ask after the welfare of those whom he had left behind, or to give counsel on points about which they had consulted him. They brim over with the expressions of a tender and heartfelt love. He is able to assure those to whom he is writing that he is praying for them, and that not only in the mass but one by one. He kept their faces and names alive in his memory by thus recalling them at the throne of grace ; and his life must have been one long prayer about his work.

Sometimes he lets the prayer which he has been offering slip through his pen ; and then we see how high was the ideal of Christian attainment which he cherished on behalf of his converts. He was not content that they had turned from their old sins and taken the first steps in the Divine life. He longed to see them becoming creditable specimens of Christianity and ornaments to the Church—complete men, thoroughly furnished unto all good works. It was life itself to him to hear of their progress : " Now we live, if ye stand fast in the Lord." And the crown to which he looked forward as the reward of all his toils and sufferings was to be permitted at last to present the soul of everyone of them as a chaste virgin to Christ.

Gentlemen, I believe that almost any preacher, on reviewing a ministry of any considerable duration, would confess that his great mistake had been the neglect of individuals. If I may be permitted a personal reference: when, not long ago, I had the opportunity, as I was passing from one charge to another, of reviewing a ministry of twelve years, the chief impression made on me, as I looked back, was that this was the point at which I had failed; and I said to myself that henceforth I would write Individuals on my heart as the watchword of my ministry.

We make impressions in the church; but we do not follow them up, to see that the decision is arrived at and the work of God accomplished; and so they are dissipated by the influences of the world; and those who have experienced them are perhaps made worse instead of better. It is a very significant thing that is said of the pastor in our Lord's parable—that he sought the lost sheep "until he found it." We seek: we even seek laboriously and painfully: but we frequently leave off just before finding.

A minister told me that, on the Saturday evening before his first Sunday in his first charge, the experienced minister who was to introduce him to his people next day was strolling with him in the vicinity of the village and talking about his duties, when they chanced to pass a plantation of trees. Pointing to them, the aged minister asked, "If you had to cut

these trees down, how would you go about it? would
you go round the whole plantation, giving each tree
a single blow, and then go round them all again,
giving each a second blow?" "Well, no," he answered, "I think I should attack one tree and cut
at it till it came down; and then go on and do the
same to a second and a third, and so forth." "Well,
said his experienced friend, "that is the way you
must do here. After you have been settled a short
time, you will discover which families and individuals
are most impressed by your first efforts, and you must
devote yourself to these susceptible souls, till you
have won them thoroughly; and then in their enthusiasm for yourself and their willingness to work for
the congregation you will have the best foundation
for a successful ministry."

In a former lecture I spoke of the power of
discerning in men and women of every class and
condition the humanity which is common to all and
speaking straight to that, without reference to the
superficial differences which distinguish class from
class and one individual from another. But ministerial sympathy has to embrace what is peculiar to
classes and individuals as well as what is common
to all. Though St. Paul, like his Master, had a
powerful grasp of what is universal in humanity, yet
to the Jew he made himself a Jew, that he might gain

the Jew, and to them that were without law as without law, that he might gain them who were without law ; he was made all things to all men, that he might gain the more.

His persuasion obviously was, that God was trying, by His revelation among those who possessed the Written Word and by His providence among those who did not possess it, to lead His children by divers ways to Himself ; and his own duty was to join himself to each company at the stage which it had reached and offer to become its conductor. The Jew was more advanced, and he met him where he was ; the Gentile was further behind, and he had to go back and approach him also where he stood, that he might win his confidence and be allowed to lead him on.

This is the persuasion which gives a minister faith in his own work. The souls of men are God's. His providence is a discipline intended to lead them to Himself ; there are none with whom His Spirit does not strive. And it is only as our work co-operates with His that it is of any effect. Where God been working, opening and softening the heart, very simple efforts, put forth at the right moment, may go a long way, and the work of God be quickly done.

What situation could be more pathetic to a sensitive

and sympathetic mind than that of a minister when he stands up in the pulpit and looks down on the congregation? What a variety of conditions are before him! In one pew there is a man who during the week has been fighting a losing battle with his business and sees himself on the verge of bankruptcy; in the next may be a merchant into whose lap fortune has been pouring her gifts in handfuls. Here is a mother who is thinking of her son who has just left his home and is sailing on the sea; and there a girl whose heart is rejoicing in the happy dreams of youth. On the right may be a young man who is trembling on the brink of the great temptation of his life, and on the left another who is reeking from some orgy of secret sin. There is endless variety; yet none are uninteresting; and probably there is no one but, if you could meet him exactly where he stands, would respond to the influence which you bring. It arrests men when you are able to show such a knowledge of the human heart that they feel themselves discovered; and it disposes a man to answer to your call if he sees that you are familiar with the circumstances in which he will have to lead the life to which you are inviting him, and that you appreciate the difficulties of the situation. Therefore the more a minister knows of the variety of actual life the better; and, if he is to do really effective work, he must know how to come down from the pulpit and put himself alongside of individuals.*

Here I might again recommend the work of visitation and the practice of being accessible at home to the visits of those who come with confidences to communicate ; but let me rather close this lecture with a word or two on some of the more favourable opportunities which ministerial life affords for direct dealing with individuals.†

One of the best opportunities of this kind is when parents come seeking baptism for their children. When you are speaking in their children's interest, men will welcome an amount of faithfulness which they would not endure at other times. You can

---

* " Get others to talk : what a man says to you has more influence upon him than all you can say to him.

"It is not the time of sickness so much as the time of convalescence that decides the future life. Remember this, and seize opportunities."— PREDIGER.

† "Much of the Gospels is taken up with conversations between Christ and individuals. Teaching so startling and difficult as His, with such an element in it of attraction and hope, naturally drew around Him many who sought to know further what this Gospel meant. He, on His part, was as eager to meet inquirers as they were to seek Him ; and we find that He bestowed as much care and pains in expounding the nature of His kingdom to individuals as He did when He was speaking to great multitudes. The audience, if small, was fit. Not only so, but we find that He put Himself in the way of individuals."—NICOLL, *The Incarnate Saviour.*

show how much their children's welfare in time and eternity may depend on their own religious condition ; you can urge the duty of family worship ; and you must have very little skill if you cannot get very close to their hearts.   Especially when a man comes about the baptism of his first child, he is perhaps in the most favourable state for an earnest talk in which you can ever find him.   His soul is opened with tenderness and overawed with the mystery of life ; he is longing with his whole heart to do his best for his child ; and, if you show him that the best he can do for it is to become connected with the great source of holy influence himself, there is no other occasion on which a good impression is more likely to be made.

The other opportunity which I should like to mention is when the young come to join the Church.   I well remember that, when I was a student, there was no part of a minister's duty to which I looked forward with so much fear and trembling as this ; for I had the conviction, which I still have, that it is our duty at this crisis to bring the question of personal salvation in the most direct and solemn way before every intending communicant, and that it is ministerial treason to let the opportunity slip.   Some of you may be looking forward to this with the same feelings ; and, therefore, I am happy to tell you that in practice it is not nearly so difficult as it seems at a distance. The applicants themselves expect you to be faithful ; if you are, they will honour you for it, and, if not, they will be disappointed. If they get the opportunity, they are far franker than you would expect. No doubt it is delicate work, and one has to guard against harshness and anything inquisitorial ; but it yields the most blessed results. This is the harvest-time of the minister's year, when he sees that his labour is not in vain. Even one such close talk, brought about in this way or otherwise, casts a glow of reality into one's work which does not pass away for weeks ; and, if a minister is so highly honoured as to receive many of these confidences, he acquires a skill in laying his finger on the very pulse of his hearers' deepest life which nothing else can give.

LECTURE IX

THE PREACHER AS A THINKER

LECTURE IX.

THE PREACHER AS A THINKER.

GENTLEMEN, in the foregoing lectures I have adverted very little to the studies, in preparation for the work of the ministry, with which you are at present occupied. Indeed, I have rather ostentatiously kept to a standpoint at some distance from the academic one, for reasons which I explained in the opening lecture. But the clue which I have endeavoured faithfully to follow has brought us at last to this point also ; and I welcome the opportunity of saying something about the more intellectual aspects of our work. The subject to-day is the Preacher as a Thinker.

In last lecture I spoke of the vast sphere of operations assigned to St. Paul and of the almost superhuman exertions which he made to fill it. But what did he exert himself to fill it with ? It was not merely to overtake the ground and be himself present in so many countries and cities that he was so zealous.

That which drove him on was the glorious message of which he was the bearer, with the sound of which he desired to fill the world. He often combines these two ideas in his writings—that the Gentile world had been committed to him as a trust, to care for the souls which it contained, and that the Gospel had been committed to him as a trust, to be communicated to the Gentiles. These two things were included in his apostolate—on the one hand, the care of the heathen world and, on the other, the publication of the Gospel.

Of course he had not, like the original apostles, heard the Gospel from the lips of Christ ; but he had received it directly from Christ in some other way ; and you know how vigorously he claimed that he had not received it from man and was not indebted to the other apostles for it. He frequently calls it his own gospel, and he maintains it to be as authentic and authoritative as that preached by any of the other apostles. How it was revealed to him we cannot tell. This is the same mystery as we encountered in study-ing the prophets of the Old Testament. Both prophets and apostles speak with a knowledge of the mind and will of God which has a certainty and authority peculiar to their writings. We ought to speak, if we speak at all, with certainty and authority too ; but there is a difference between ours and theirs.

I know how difficult it is to define the difference ; we cover it up with the vague word Inspiration ; but I do not see any use in hiding from ourselves that it exists.

Admitting, however, that there is this mystery, yet we can see, in some respects, how the truth, when it came, dealt with St. Paul, and how his mind was exercised about it ; and in these respects he is not beyond our imitation.

What I wish to emphasize in this lecture is, that Christianity did specially lay hold of him in the region of the intellect. It is meant to lay hold of all parts of the inner man—the feelings, the conscience, the will, the intellect ; and it may lay hold of certain people more fully in one part of their being and of others in another according to their constitutional peculiarities. Some suppose—and perhaps they are not far wrong—that the first preaching of the Gospel consisted of little more than the simple story of the life and death of Jesus ; that those who heard it sympathetically began forthwith to live new lives in imitation of Christ ; and that this was the most of their Christianity. In a fine and peculiar nature like that of St. John, again, the Gospel caught hold chiefly in the region of the emotions ; and his Christianity was a mystical union and fellowship between the Saviour and the soul. St. Paul was not by any means

16

deficient in the other elements of humanity ; but he was conspicuously strong in intellect. That is to say, he was one of those natures to which it is a necessity to know the why and the wherefore of everything—of the universe in which they live, of the experiences through which they pass, of the ends which they are called upon to pursue. This natural tendency was strengthened by the training of an educated man. And therefore the Gospel came to him as a message of truth, which cleared up the mysteries of existence and presented the universe to the mind as a realm of order.

St. Paul often expresses the intense intellectual satisfaction which Christianity brought him, and the joy he experienced in applying it to the solution of the problems of life. The light which Christianity cast on the universe was to him, he says, like the morning of creation, when God said, Let there be light, and there was light. Before, all was darkness and chaos, but then all became sunshine and order. He often speaks with wondering gratitude of the fact that the mystery which had been hidden from ages and from generations had been revealed to him : Eye had not seen, nor ear heard, neither had entered into the heart of man, the things which God had prepared for them that love Him, but God had revealed them unto him by His Spirit. And by this mystery he meant the tangle of God's providence in history, which the coming of Christ disentangled and smoothed out into a web whose pattern the mind could discern.

Having himself received Christianity as an intellectual system, he very specially addressed himself to the intellect of others. The door of the kingdom of heaven, it has been beautifully said, can only be opened from the inside ; but to that observation this other may be added, that in a sense there are many doors, but each man can only open to others the one by which he has entered himself. Christianity had come to St. Paul as the truth about God and the world and himself. There was plenty of emotion besides ; but the emotion for him came after the clear intellectual conviction and sprang out of it. And he expected that others would receive Christianity in the same way. Therefore he never spared the minds of those he addressed ; he expected them to think ; and he would have said that, if they would not open and exert their minds, they could not receive Christianity.

I hardly know anything more puzzling than the audacity with which he cast himself on the minds of his hearers and trusted them to understand him, when he was thinking his strongest and his deepest. Imagine an epistle of his arriving in Rome or Ephesus,

and read out in the audience of the church for the
first time. Who were the hearers? The majority
of them were slaves; many had till a short time
before been unconcerned about religion; in all probability not a tithe of them could read or write. Yet
what did Paul give them? Not milk for babes; not
a compost of stories and practical remarks; but the
Epistle to the Romans, with its strict logic and
grand ideas, or the Epistle to the Ephesians, with its
involved sentences and profound mysticism. He
must have believed that they would understand
what he wrote, though scholarship has considered
it necessary to pile up a mountain of commentaries
on these epistles. Christianity, as it went through
the cities of the world in St. Paul's person, must have
gone as a great intellectual awakening, which taught
men to use their minds in investigating the pro-
foundest problems of life.

How deeply he was interested in the intellectual
reception of the Gospel is shown by the earnestness
with which he prays that his converts may excel in
mental grasp of the truth. "I pray," he says, "that
your love may abound yet more and more in knowledge and in all judgment." And again he says,
"Making mention of you in my prayers, that the
God of our Lord Jesus Christ, the Father of glory,
may give unto you the spirit of wisdom and revela-

tion in the knowledge of Him, the eyes of your understanding being enlightened," etc.

But nothing proves so clearly the value which he set on this element of Christianity as his earnestness that his version of the Gospel should be kept pure and entire. He called upon younger ministers, like Timothy and Titus, to guard it as a precious treasure and to transmit it to faithful men who would be able to teach others also. It filled him with the most poignant anxiety and pain when the minds of his converts were assailed with doctrines subversive of the truth which he had taught. He had to encounter assaults of this kind coming from the side of orthodoxy as well as of heterodoxy, and no small portion of his energy had to be expended in refuting them. You remember, for example, with what a heat of zeal and affection he cast himself on the Galatians, when they had lent an ear to false teachers : " O foolish Galatians, who hath bewitched you ? " " If any man preach any other gospel unto you than that which ye have received, let him be accursed."

Gentlemen, you are going to be teachers of Christianity, and this implies that you should yourselves have mastered it in thought. A certain number of people will be more or less dependent on you for the view they have of Christianity ; and this really means the view they have of all the most important and solemn objects of existence; for to them all things will be comprehended in Christianity; and on you will largely depend whether this view is true or false, narrow or noble.

It would be difficult to exaggerate the importance to men and women of their fundamental convictions about this universe in which they live. There is current, indeed, at present a way of speaking about the intellect, as if, while all the other faculties have to do with religion, it were only an intruder; and there is a way of speaking about definite religious truth which really implies, if any strict meaning is to be attached to it, that in religion, when the truth is not found, the opposite may answer quite as well; and yet, strange to say, this language is usually to be heard from the lips of those who make special claims to intellectuality and affect to be the special champions of truth. But the intellect is a noble faculty and has an important office in religion. It is, properly speaking, antecedent to both feeling and will; and what is put into it determines both what feeling and choice will be. People are often, indeed, swept into the Church on some current of feeling; and the pressure on every side of the Christian society, along with the examples of superior Christians, does much to develop the religious nature; but probably in the great crises of temptation, when a flood of passion or some great worldly opportunity is about to sweep a man away from his connection with Christ, that which keeps hold of him is the force of conviction—if the roots of his mind have gone deep down and clasped themselves about the great verities of the faith. Our Lord Himself called the truth the foundation on which the whole structure of life is built. All that a man is and does depends, in the last resort, on what he knows and believes. It will be a calamity for your hearers, if from your preaching they are not able by degrees to put together in their minds a conception of Christianity both true and elevating, which will supply them with the fundamental principles of their life.

Besides this sacred obligation to our people, there is the obligation to the truth itself. This was felt by St. Paul profoundly. A revelation of Christianity had been committed to him, and he had to present it in all its splendour and apply it to all the details of life. So the Word of God is committed to us, and we are responsible for delivering its whole message. If we take up a single text of the Bible, our merit as preachers lies in bringing out attractively and comprehensively the truth which it contains. It would be considered still more meritorious to present the whole message contained in a book of the Bible;

and it would be quite in accordance with the theological fashion of the time if a preacher were able to show that he was master of some single section of Scripture, say, the Prophets of the Old Testament or the writings of St. John. I do not know why we should hesitate about the next step, which, if we have gone so far, we are logically bound to take—the mastery of the message of the Bible as a whole. This is what we are responsible for. The Bible is the message of the mind and will of the loving and redeeming God; and this we are bound to deliver in such a way that neither its truth nor its glory will suffer in our hands.

How this is to be done, of course it requires wisdom to decide, and there will doubtless be different ways for different men and for different times. In a former generation a president of this college* preached in the College Chapel straight through the doctrines of Christianity, taking them up one by one in systematic order; and his book was long a model to preachers both in this country and Great Britain. He was preaching to an academic audience, and there are probably few congregations for which such a course would be suitable now; although I know at least one able young minister in a country

---

* President Dwight.

village who has been pursuing this method from the commencement of his ministry. Once a month he gives a sermon of the course; perhaps his people do do not know that he is doing so; but he is giving his own mind the discipline of investigating the doctrines of Christianity in their order; and I am certain both that he himself is growing a strong man in the process and that his people, though unconsciously, are getting the benefit of it. In the Lutheran and Episcopal Churches the observance of the Christian festivals gives occasion for regularly bringing the circle of the grand Christian facts before the minds of the people. We have not this guidance; but a faithful minister is bound to make sure that he is preaching with sufficient frequency on the leading Christian facts and doctrines, and that he is not omitting any essential element of Christianity.*

Not unfrequently ministers are exhorted to cultivate extreme simplicity in their preaching. Everything ought, we are told, to be brought down to the comprehension of the most ignorant hearer, and even of children. Far be it from me to depreciate the place of the simplest in the congregation; it is one of the best features of the Church of the present day that

---

* "Great subjects insure solid thinking. Solid thinking prompts a sensible style, an athletic style, on some themes a magnificent style, and on all themes a natural style."—PHELPS, *My Note-book.*

it cares for the lambs. I dealt with this subject, not unsympathetically I hope, in a former lecture. But do not ask us to be always speaking to children or to beginners. Is the Bible always simple? Is Job simple, or Isaiah? Is the Epistle to the Romans simple, or Galatians? This cry for simplicity is three-fourths intellectual laziness ; and that Church is doomed in which there is not supplied meat for men as well as milk for babes. We owe the Gospel not only to the barbarian but also to the Greek, not only to the unwise but also to the wise.*

I do not believe, however, that it is only in cultured congregations that this element of preaching is required. There is no greater mistake than to suppose that you will drive the common man away from the Church by strong intellectual preaching. You will do so no doubt if you preach over his head,† and use a

---

* "We owe it to the Church, we owe it to the time in which God has called us to labour, we owe it to the restless and perplexed but often honest minds in whose presence we carry on our ministry, to be not merely a hard-working but a learned clergy. To those great questions which both stir and disquiet men, we are bound to bring that knowledge which will give us a claim to be listened to. 'Know as much as you can ; ' that ought to be the rule to which an educated clergyman should hold himself for ever tied. A clergyman ought to be a *student*, a reader and a thinker, to the very end."—DEAN CHURCH.

† Richard Baxter confesses that he deliberately preached over the heads of his people once a year, for the purpose of keeping them humble and showing them what their minister could do every Sunday of the year, if he chose !

language which he does not understand. You must find him where he is, and either speak to him in his own language or teach him yours by slow degrees. But, if you accommodate yourself to him so far, you will find him alert and willing to accompany you; you will find that he has not only sturdy limbs for climbing, but even wings for soaring to the heights of truth.

A greater difficulty lies in the preacher himself. At the beginning of his ministry he may be encumbered with doubts and far from clear in his faith. This is a real obstacle, and the first years of ministerial life may be a time of great perplexity and pain. I suspect our congregations have often a good deal to suffer while we are endeavouring to preach ourselves clear. It is vicarious suffering; for they do not know what is perplexing us. They have to stand by and look on while their minister is fighting his doubts. But, if he is a true man, it is worth their while to wait. If these are the pangs of intellectual birth, and the truth is merely divesting itself of a traditional form in order to invest itself in a form which is his own, he will preach with far greater power when the process is complete, and he is able to speak with the strength of personal conviction.

But, gentlemen, it is important for you to see that your opening ministry is not enveloped in mist simply because you have never made a real study of Christianity. This, I am afraid, is the commonest source of a vague theology. In a former lecture I have recommended a wide acquaintance with the masterpieces of literature ; but some able men at college substitute this for the studies of their profession ; and this is a fatal mistake. Literature ought to be a supplement to these, not a substitute for them. I have watched the subsequent career of more than one student who had pursued this course ; and I must say it is not encouraging. Their supply of ideas soon runs out ; their tone becomes secular ; and the people turn away from them dissatisfied.

A student ought, while at College, to make himself master of at least one or two of the great books of the Christian centuries in which Christianity is exhibited as a whole by a master mind. If I may be allowed to mention my own experience, it happened to me, more by chance, perhaps, than wise choice, to master, when I was a student, three such books. One was Owen's work on *The Holy Spirit*, another Weiss' *New Testament Theology*, and the third Conybeare and Howson's *Life and Epistles of St. Paul.* Each of these may be said, in its own way, to exhibit Christianity entire, and I learned them almost by heart, as one does a text-book. I was not then thinking much of subsequent benefit ; but I can say, that each of them has ever since been a quarry out of which I have dug, and probably I have hardly ever preached a sermon which has not exhibited traces of their influence.

There is another valuable result which will follow from the early mastery of books of this kind. You will be laying the foundation of the habit of what may be called Great Reading, by which I mean the systematic study of great theological works in addition to the special reading for the work of each Sunday. Week by week a conscientious minister has to do an immense amount of miscellaneous reading in commentaries, dictionaries, etc., in connection with the discourses in hand; but, in addition to this, he should be enriching the subsoil of his mind by larger efforts in wider fields. It is far from easy to carry this on in a busy pastorate; and it is almost impossible unless the foundation has been laid at college.*

One more hint I should like to give: it is a reminiscence from a casual lecture which I listened to when a student and profited by. Besides attending to theological studies in general, one ought to have a specialty. The minister, and even the student before

---

* "A sentence of Pascal would sometimes shoot more light and life through a sermon than all the commentators upon the text since the days of Noah."—PRINCIPAL RAINY.

he leaves college, should be spoken of as the man who knows this or that. Perhaps the best specialty to choose is some subject which is just coming into notice, such as, at present, Comparative Religion, or Christian Ethics, or, best of all, Biblical Theology. Such a speciality, early taken up, is like a well dug on one's property, which year by year becomes deeper. All the little streams and rivulets of reading and experience find their way into it; and almost unawares the happy possessor comes to have within himself a fountain which makes it impossible that his mind should ever run dry.

Of course I cannot attempt to give here even the slightest sketch of the doctrinal system of St. Paul; but there are two characteristics of it which I should like to mention in closing, as they are essential to the right management of the element of preaching with which I have occupied you to-day.

1. The thinking of St. Paul went hand in hand with his experience. His Christianity began in a great experience, in which he discovered the secret of life and found peace with God. He set his mind to reflect upon this, so as to comprehend how it came about and what it involved; and the theology of the first part of his apostolate was nothing but the result of these broodings under the guidance

of the Holy Spirit. These in their turn, however, brought him still nearer to God and closer to Christ; and so he obtained new and deeper experiences, of which the doctrines of his more advanced life are again the exposition. Thus his thinking was both experimental and progressive. If his Epistles be arranged in chronological order, it will easily be seen that there is a splendid growth in his theology from first to last. He never, indeed, gave up the doctrines of his earlier life; there is no inconsistency between one part of his writings and another; but neither his experience nor his thinking ever stood still; he made his first doctrines the foundations on which he reared a structure which was rising higher and higher to the very close of his life.

St. Paul had the heartiest scorn for intellectualism in religion divorced from experience; and it cannot be denied that it is this divorce which has brought contempt on the intellectual element in preaching. When doctrine is preached as mere dogma, imposed as a form on the mind of the preacher from without, no wonder it is dry and barren. It is when the preacher's own experience is growing, and he is coming up with the doctrines of Christianity one by one as the natural expression for what he knows in his deepest consciousness to be true, that he utters the truth with power. Never, perhaps, is a sermon so living as when the preacher has found out the truth during the week as a novelty to himself, and comes forth on Sunday to deliver it with the joy of discovery.

2. The other feature to which I wish to draw attention is the perfect balance in St. Paul of the doctrinal and the ethical. If reproach has been cast on the intellectual element in preaching by its want of connection with experience, this has been done no less by its want of connection with conduct. But St. Paul is not open to this reproach. This is made clear by the very external form of his writings. An Epistle of St. Paul is divided into two parts, the first containing doctrines and the second practical rules for the conduct of life ; and not unfrequently the two parts are of about equal length.

But the connection is far closer than this. In St. Paul's mind all the great doctrines of the Gospel were living fountains of motives for well-doing ; and even the smallest and commonest duties of every-day life were magnified and made sacred by being connected with the facts of salvation. Take a single instance. There is no plainer duty of every-day life than telling the truth. Well, how does St. Paul treat it ? "Lie not one to another," he says, " seeing ye have put off the old man with his deeds." Thus truthfulness flows out of regeneration. Treating of the same subject again, he says, " Lie not one to another, for ye are members one of another," deriving the duty from the union of believers to one another through their common union with Christ.* Thus does St. Paul everywhere show great principles in small duties and stamp the commonest actions of life with the image and the superscription of Christ.

This balance between the doctrinal and the moral is difficult to maintain. Seldom has the mind of the Church been able to preserve it for any length of time. It has oscillated from one kind of one-sidedness to another, sometimes exalting doctrines and neglecting duties and at other times preaching up morality and disparaging doctrine. To which side

* Rev. Dr. Henderson, of Crieff, told me a story which illustrates in an amusing yet significant way the change which passed over the religious mind of Scotland in the beginning of the present century. His father, the late Rev. Dr. Henderson, of Glasgow, when a young minister, was preaching, on the Saturday before a communion, for an extremely Moderate minister of the dignified and pompous school. "I do not know, Mr. Henderson," said the latter, "what is the difference between you Evangelicals and us ; but I suppose it is that you preach doctrines, while we preach duties." "I do not know about that," said Mr. Henderson ; "we preach duties too." "Well," said the old man, "for example, my action sermon to-morrow is to be on lying ; and my divisions are—first, the nature of lying ; secondly, the sin of lying ; and thirdly, the consequences of lying: now what could you add to that ? "Well," replied Mr. Henderson, "I would add two things—first, 'Lie not one to another, seeing ye have put off the old man with his deeds,' and secondly, 'Putting away lying, speak every man truth with his neighbour ; for we are members one of another.'" "Mr. Henderson, these suggestions are admirable : I shall add them to my discourse !"

the balance may be dipping at the present time among you I do not know; but among us, I should say, it is from doctrines towards duties.

Perhaps in the last generation we had too much preaching of doctrine, or rather I should say, too little preaching of duty. Younger preachers are beginning to dwell much on a nobler conception of the Christian life, and there is a strong demand for practical preaching. Undoubtedly there is room for a healthy development in this direction. Yet this is a transition about which our country has good cause to be jealous; because it passed through a terrible experience of the effects of preaching morality without doctrine. I question if in the whole history of the pulpit there is a document more worthy of the attention of preachers than the address which Dr. Chalmers sent to the people of his first charge at Kilmeny, when he was leaving it for Glasgow. It is well known that for seven years after his settlement in this rural parish he was ignorant of the Gospel and preached only the platitudes of the Moderate creed; but, the grace of God having visited his heart, he lived for other five years among his people as a true ambassador of Christ, beseeching them in Christ's name to be reconciled to God. This is his summing up of the results of the two periods :—

" And here I cannot but record the effect of an

actual though undesigned experiment, which I prose-
cuted for upwards of twelve years among you. For
the greater part of that time I could expatiate on
the meanness of dishonesty, on the villany of falsehood, on the despicable arts of calumny ; in a word,
upon all those deformities of character which awaken
the natural indignation of the human heart against
the pests and the disturbers of human society. Now,
could I, upon the strength of these warm expostu-
lations, have got the thief to give up his stealing, and
the evil speaker his censoriousness, and the liar his
deviations from truth, I should have felt all the
repose of one who had gotten his ultimate object.
It never occurred to me that all this might have been
done, and yet the soul of every hearer have remained
in full alienation from God ; and that, even could I
have established in the bosom of one who stole such
a principle of abhorrence at the meanness of dishonesty that he was prevailed upon to steal no more,
he might still have retained a heart as completely
unturned to God and as totally unpossessed by a
principle of love to Him as before. In a word, though
I might have made him a more upright and honourable
man, I might have left him as destitute of the essence
of religious principle as ever. But the interesting
fact is, that during the whole of that period in which
I made no attempt against the natural enmity of

the mind to God ; while I was inattentive to the way in which this enmity is dissolved, even by the free offer on the one hand, and the believing acceptance on the other, of the Gospel salvation ; while Christ, through whose blood the sinner, who by nature stands afar off, is brought near to the heavenly Lawgiver, whom he has offended, was scarcely ever spoken of, or spoken of in such a way as stripped Him of all the importance of His character and His offices ; even at this time I certainly did press the reformations of honour and truth, and integrity among my people ; but I never once heard of any such reformations having been effected amongst them. If there was anything at all brought about in this way, it was more than ever I got any account of. I am not sensible that all the vehemence with which I urged the virtues and the proprieties of social life had the weight of a feather on the moral habits of my parishioners. And it was not till I got impressed by the utter alienation of the heart in all its desires and affections from God ; it was not till reconciliation to Him became the distinct and the prominent object of my ministerial exertions ; it was not till I took the Scriptural way of laying the method of reconciliation before them ; it was not till the free offer of forgiveness through the blood of Christ was urged upon their acceptance, and the Holy Spirit, given through the channel of Christ's mediatorship to all who ask Him, was set before them as the unceasing object of their dependence and their prayers ; in one word, it was not till the contemplations of my people were turned to these great and essential elements in the business of a soul providing for its interest with God and the concerns of its eternity, that I ever heard of any of those subordinate reformations which I aforetime made the earnest and the zealous, but, I am afraid, at the same time the ultimate object of my earlier ministrations. Ye servants, whose scrupulous fidelity has now attracted the notice, and drawn forth in my hearing a delightful testimony from your masters, what mischief you would have done, had your zeal for doctrines and sacraments been accompanied by the sloth and the remissness, and what, in the prevailing tone of moral relaxation, is counted the allowable purloining of your earlier days. But a sense of your Heavenly Master's eye has brought another influence to bear upon you ; and, while you are thus striving to adorn the doctrine of God your Saviour in all things, you may, poor as you are, reclaim the great ones of the land to the acknowledgment of the faith. You have at least taught me that to preach Christ is the only effective way of preaching morality in all its branches ; and out of your humble cottages have I gathered a lesson, which I pray God

I may be enabled to carry with all its simplicity into a wider theatre, and to bring with all the power of its subduing efficacy upon the vices of a more crowded population."

There is nothing which I should more like to leave ringing in your ears than this remarkable statement of my great fellow-countryman. But I cannot close and bid you farewell without expressing the happiness which I have derived from these weeks spent in your society and thanking you for the extremely encouraging attendance with which you have honoured me from first to last. To the authorities of the college, as well as many citizens of this town, I have to express my indebtedness for an amount of kindness and courtesy which I can never forget, and which will always make my visit to this country one of the pleasantest of memories.

Let us, in parting, commend each other to the grace of God :

O God our Father, the infinite Power, the perfect Wisdom and the immortal Love, in Thy hands are all our ways, and the success of our purposes proceeds from Thee alone. Follow with Thy blessing our intercourse together and the work which we have now completed. Bless this University—its president, its professors and students. May knowledge grow in it from more to more, and, along with knowledge, reverence and love. May those especially who are preparing for the ministry of Thy Son be filled with Thy Spirit, and in due time may they prove faithful stewards of the mysteries of God. Bless them in their studies, in their fellowship with one another, and in their efforts to advance Thy kingdom. We commend each other affectionately to Thee ; be our God and our Guide in life and in death, in time and in eternity. For Christ's sake. Amen.

APPENDIX

AN ORDINATION CHARGE

APPENDIX.

AN ORDINATION CHARGE.*

I SHOULD like to connect what I have to say with a text of Scripture, which you may remember as a motto for this occasion. Take, then, that pastoral exhortation to a young minister in 1 Tim. iv. 16: "Take heed unto thyself, and to the doctrine; continue in them; for in doing this thou shalt both save thyself and them that hear thee."

There are three subjects recommended in this text to one in your position—*first*, yourself; *second*, your doctrine; and *third*, those that hear you.

I. *Take heed unto thyself.*—Perhaps there is no profession which so thoroughly as ours tests and reveals what is in a man—the stature of his manhood, the mass and quality of his character, the poverty or richness of his mind, the coldness or warmth of his

---

* Delivered at the Ordination of the Rev. William Agnew, Gallatown, Kirkcaldy, 1879.

spirituality. These all come out in our work, and become known to our congregation and the community in which we labour.

When a man comes into a neighbourhood, as you are doing now, he is to a large extent an unknown quantity; and it is very touching to observe the exaggeration with which we are generally looked on at first, people attributing to us a sort of indefinite largeness. But it is marvellous how soon the measure of a man is taken, how he finds his level in the community, and people know whether he is a large or a petty man, whether he is a thinker or not, whether he is a deeply religious man or not. The glamour of romance passes off, and everything is seen in the light of common day.

The sooner this takes place the better. A true man does not need to fear it. He is what he is, and nothing else. He cannot by taking thought add one cubit to his stature. Any exaggeration of his image in the minds of others does not in reality make him one inch bigger than he is.

It seems to me to lie at the very root of a right ministerial life to be possessed with this idea—to get quit of everything like pretence and untruthfulness, to wish for no success to which one is not entitled, and to look upon elevation into any position for which one is unfit as a pure calamity.

The man's self—the very thing he is, standing with his bare feet on the bare earth—this is the great concern. This is the self to which you are to take heed—what you really are, what you are growing to, what you may yet become.

All our work is determined by this—the spirit and power of our preaching, the quality of the influence we exert, and the tenor of our walk and conversation. We can no more rise above ourselves than water can rise above its own level. We may, indeed, often fail to do ourselves justice, and sometimes may do ourselves more than justice. But that is only for a moment; the total impression made by ourselves is an unmistakeable thing. What is in us must come out, and nothing else. All we say and do is merely the expression of what we are.

Evidently, therefore, there can be nothing so important as carefully to watch over our inner life, and see that it be large, sweet and spiritual, and that it be growing.

Yet the temptations to neglect and overlook this and turn our attention in other directions are terribly strong. The ministerial life is a very outside life; it is lived in the glare of publicity; it is always pouring out. We are continually preaching, addressing meetings, giving private counsel, attending public gatherings, going from home, frequenting church

courts, receiving visits, and occupied with details of
every kind. We live in a time when all men are
busy, and ministers are the busiest of men. From
Monday morning till Sunday night the bustle goes
on continually.

Our life is in danger of becoming *all* outside. We
are called upon to express ourselves before conviction
has time to ripen. Our spirits get too hot and un-
settled to allow the dew to fall on them. We are
compelled to speak what is merely the recollection of
conviction which we had some time ago, and to use
past feeling over again. Many a day you will feel
this; you will long with your whole heart to escape
away somewhere into obscurity, and be able to keep
your mouth closed for weeks. You will know the
meaning of that great text for ministers, "The talk of
the lips tendeth only to penury,"—that is, it shallows
the spirit within.

This is what we have to fight against. The people
we live among and the hundred details of our calling
will steal away our inner life altogether, if they can.
And then, what is our outer life worth? It is worth
nothing. If the inner life get thin and shallow, the
outer life must become a perfunctory discharge of
duties. Our preaching will be empty, and our conversation and intercourse unspiritual, unenriching and
flavourless. We may please our people for a time by

doing all they desire and being at everybody's call ; but they will turn round on us in disappointment and anger in the day when, by living merely the outer life, we have become empty, shallow and unprofitable.

Take heed to thyself! If we grow strong and large inwardly, our people will reap the fruit of it in due time : our preaching will have sap and power and unction ; and our intercourse will have about it the breath of another world .

We *must* find time for reading, study, meditation and prayer. We should at least insist on having a large forenoon, up, say, to two o'clock every day, clear of interruptions. These hours of quietness are our real life ! It is these that make the ministerial life a grand life. When we are shut in alone, and, the spirit having been silenced and collected by prayer, the mind gets slowly down into the heart of a text, like a bee in a flower, it is like heaven upon earth ; it is as if the soul were bathing itself in morning dews ; the dust and fret are washed off, and the noises recede into the distance ; peace comes ; we move aloft in another world—the world of ideas and realities ; the mind mounts joyfully from one height to another ; it sees the common world far beneath, yet clearly, in its true meaning and size and relations to other worlds. And then one comes down on Sabbath, to speak to the people, calm, strong and clear, like Moses from the mount, and with a true Divine message.

In so doing, my dear brother, thou shalt save thyself. Lose your inner life, and you lose yourself, sure enough ; for that *is* yourself. You will often have to tell your people that salvation is not the one act of conversion, nor the one act of passing through the gate of heaven at last ; but the renewal, the sanctification, the growth, into large and symmetrical stature, of the whole character. Tell that to yourself often too. We take it for granted that you are a regenerated man, or we would not have ordained you to be a minister of the Gospel to-day. But it is possible for a man to be regenerate and to be a minister, and yet to remain very worldly, shallow, undeveloped and unsanctified. We who are your brethren in the ministry could tell sad histories in illustration of this out of our own inner life. We could tell you how, in keeping the vineyard of others, we have often neglected our own ; and how now, at the end of years of ministerial activity and incessant toil, we turn round and look with dismay at our shallow characters, our unenriched minds, and our lack of spirituality and Christlikeness. O brother ! take heed to thyself— save thyself !

II. *Take heed to the Doctrine.*—A very little expe-

rience of preaching will convince you that in relation
to the truth which you have to minister week by week
to your people you will have to sustain a double
character—that of an interpreter of Scripture and
that of a prophet.

Let me first say something of the former. With
whatever high-flown notions a man may begin his
ministry, yet, if he is to stay for years in a place and
keep up a fresh kind of preaching and build up a
congregation, delivering such discourses as Scotchmen
like to hear, he will find that he must heartily accept
the *rôle* of an interpreter of Scripture, and lean on the
Bible as his great support.

This is your work ; the Book is put into your
hands to-day, that you may unfold its contents to
your people, conveying them into their minds by all
possible avenues and applying them to all parts of
their daily life.

It is a grand task. I cannot help congratulating
you on being ordained to the ministry to-day, for this
above everything, that the Bible is henceforth to be
continually in your hands ; that the study of it is to
be the work of your life ; that you are to be continually sinking and bathing your mind in its truths ;
and that you are to have the pleasure of bringing
forth what you have discovered in it to feed the
minds of men. The ministerial profession is to be

18

envied more for this than anything else. I promise you that, if you be true to it, this Book will become dearer to you every day ; it will enrich every part of your nature ; you will become more and more convinced that it is the Word of God and contains the only remedy for the woes of man.

But be true to it! The Bible will be what I have said to you only if you go deep into it. If you keep to the surface, you will weary of it. There are some ministers who begin their ministry with a certain quantity of religious doctrine in their mind, and what they do all their life afterwards is to pick out texts and make them into vessels to hold so much of it. The vessels are of different shapes and sizes, but they are all filled with the same thing ; and oh! it is poor stuff, however orthodox and evangelical it may seem.

To become a dearly loved friend and an endless source of intellectual and spiritual delight, the Bible must be thoroughly studied. We must not pour our ideas into it, but apply our minds to it and faithfully receive the impressions which it makes on them. One learns thus to trust the Bible as an inexhaustible resource and lean back upon it with all one's might. It is only such preaching, enriching itself out of the wealth of the Bible and getting from it freshness, variety and power, that can build up a congregation and satisfy the minds of really living Christians.

The intellectual demand on the pulpit is rapidly rising. I should like to draw your earnest attention to a revolution which is silently taking place in Scotland but is receiving from very few the notice which it deserves. I refer to the changes that are being made by the new system of national education. No one can have travelled much for several years past through this part of the island without his attention being attracted by the new and imposing school buildings rising in almost every parish. These are the index of a revolution ; for inside, in their management and in the efficiency of the education, there has also been an immense change. I venture to say that nothing which has taken place in Scotland this century— and I am remembering both the Reform Bill and the Disruption—will be found to have been of more importance. There will be a far more educated Scotland to preach to in a short time, which will demand of the ministry a high intellectual standard. It is a just demand. Our people should go away from the church feeling that they have received new and interesting information, that their intellects have been illuminated by fresh and great ideas, and that to hear their minister regularly is a liberal education.

Nothing will meet this demand except thorough study of Scripture by minds equipped with all the technical helps, as well as enriched by the constant reading of the best literature, both on our own and kindred subjects. One of our hymns says that the Bible "gives a light to every age ; it gives, but borrows none." Nothing could be more untrue. The Bible borrows light from every age and from every department of human knowledge. Whatever especially makes us acquainted with the mysterious depths of human nature is deserving of our attention. The Bible and human nature call to each other like deep unto deep. Every addition to our knowledge of man will be a new key to open the secrets of the Word ; and the deeper you go in your preaching into the mysteries of the Word, the more subtle and powerful will be the springs you touch in the minds and hearts of your hearers.

But preparation of this sort for the pulpit is not easy. It requires time, self-conquest and hard work. Perhaps the greatest ministerial temptation is idleness in study—not in going about and doing something, but in finding and rightly using precious hours in one's library, avoiding reverie and light or desultory reading, and sticking hard and fast to the Sabbath work. I, for one, must confess that I have had, and still have, a terrible battle to fight for this. No men have their time so much at their own disposal as we. I often wish we had regular office-hours, like business men ; but even that would not remedy the evil, for every man shut up alone in a study is not studying. Nothing can remedy it but faithfulness to duty and love of work.

You will find it necessary to be hard at it from Tuesday morning to Saturday night. If you lecture, as I trust you will—for it brings one, far more than sermonising, into contact with Scripture—you will know your subject at once, and be able to begin to read on it. The text of the other discourse should be got by the middle of the week at latest, and the more elaborate of the two finished on Friday. This makes a hard week; but it has its reward. There are few moods more splendid than a preacher's when, after a hard week's work, during which his mind has been incessantly active on the truth of God and his spirit exalted by communion with the Divine Spirit, he appears before his congregation on Sabbath, knowing he has an honestly gotten message to lavish on them; just as there can be no coward and craven more abject than a minister with any conscience who appears in the pulpit after an idle, dishonest week, to cheat his congregation with a diet of fragments seasoned with counterfeit fervour.

But, besides being an interpreter of Scripture, a true minister fills the still higher position of a prophet. This congregation has asked you to become their spiritual overseer. But a minister is no minister unless he come to his sphere of labour under a far higher sanction—unless he be sent from God, with a message in his heart which he is burning to pour forth upon men. An apostle (that is, a messenger sent from God) and a prophet (that is, a man whose lips are impatient to speak the Divine message which his heart is full of) every true minister must be. I trust you have such a message, the substance of which you could at this moment, if called upon, speak out in very few words. There is something wrong if from a man's preaching his hearers do not gather by degrees a scheme of doctrine—a message which the plainest of them could give account of.

What this message should be, there exists no doubt at all in the Church of which you have to-day been ordained a minister. It can be nothing else than the evangelical scheme, as it has been understood and expounded by the greatest and most godly minds in all generations of the Church and preached with fresh power in his country since the beginning of the present century. It has proved itself the power of God, to the revival of the Church and the conversion of souls, wherever it has been faithfully proclaimed ; and it is a great trust which is committed to your hands to-day to be one of its heralds and conservators.

Not that we in this generation are to pledge ourselves to preach nothing except what was preached last generation. That would be a poor way of following in the footsteps of men who thought so independently and so faithfully fulfilled their own task. The area of topics introduced in the pulpit is widening, I think. Why should it not? The Bible is far greater and wider than any school or any generation; and we will fearlessly commit ourselves to it and go wherever it carries us, even though it should be far beyond the range of topics within which we are expected to confine ourselves. Your congregation will put one utterance side by side with another; and, if you are a truly evangelical man, there will be no fear of their mistaking your standpoint. There is no kind of preaching so wearisome and unprofitable as an anxious, constrained and formal repetition of the most prominent points of evangelical doctrine. The only cure for this is to keep in close contact with both human nature and the Bible, and be absolutely faithful to the impressions which they make.

Yet take heed that your doctrine be such as will save them that hear you. What saving doctrine is has been determined in this land by a grand experiment; and it is only faithfulness to the history of Scotland, as well as to God and your people, to make it the sum and substance and the very breath of life of all your preaching. Our calling is emphatically

" the ministry of reconciliation ; to wit, that God was in Christ, reconciling the world unto Himself, not imputing their trespasses unto them ; and hath committed unto us the word of reconciliation. Now then we are ambassadors for Christ, as though God did beseech you by us ; we pray you in Christ's stead, be ye reconciled to God. For He hath made Him to be sin for us who knew no sin ; that we might be made the righteousness of God in Him." This is the glorious message of the Gospel, which alone can meet the deep spiritual wants of men.

Preach it out of a living experience. Bunyan, in his autobiography, gives an account of his own preaching, telling how, for the first two years of his ministry, he dwelt continually on the terrors of the law, because he was then quailing beneath them himself; how for the next two years he discoursed chiefly on Christ in His offices, because he was then enjoying the comfort of these doctrines ; and how, for a third couple of years, the mystery of union to Christ was the centre both of his preaching and his experience ; and so on. That appears to me the very model of a true ministry—to be always preaching the truth one is experiencing oneself at the time, and so giving it out fresh, like a discovery just made ; while at the same time the centre of gravity, so to speak, of one's doctrine is constantly in motion, passing from one section of the sphere of evangelical truth to another, till it has in succession passed through them all.

III. *Take heed to them that hear you.*—I almost envy you the new joy that will fill your heart soon, when you fairly get connected with your congregation. The first love of a minister for his own flock is as original and peculiar a blossom of the heart as any other that could be named. And the bond that unites him to those whom he has been the means of converting or raising to higher levels of life is one of the tenderest in existence.

You have come to a hearty people, who will be quite disposed to put a good construction on all you do. This is a busy community, that appreciates a man who works hard. If you do your work faithfully and preach with the heart and the head, they will come to hear you. It is wonderful how lenient those who hear us are. You will wonder, I daresay, some Sabbaths, that they sit to hear you at all, or that, having heard you, they ever come back again. But, if a man is really true, he is not condemned for a single poor sermon. Honesty and thorough work and good thinking are not so easily found in the world that a man who generally exhibits them can be neglected. If we fail, it must surely generally be our own fault.

The more we put ourselves on a level with the

people the better. We stoop to conquer. It is
better to feel that we belong to the congregation than
that it belongs to us. I like to think of the minister
as only one of the congregation set apart by the rest
for a particular purpose. A congregation is a
number of people associated for their moral and
spiritual improvement. And they say to one of their
number, Look, brother, we are busy with our daily
toils and confused with domestic and worldly cares ;
we live in confusion and darkness ; but we eagerly
long for peace and light to cheer and illuminate our
life ; and we have heard there is a land where these
are to be found—a land of repose and joy, full of
thoughts that breathe and words that burn : but we
cannot go thither ourselves ; we are too embroiled in
daily cares : come, we will elect you, and set you free
from our toils, and you shall go thither for us, and
week by week trade with that land and bring us its
treasures and its spoils. Oh, woe to him who accepts
this election, and yet, failing through idleness to
carry on the noble merchandise, appears week by
week empty-handed or with merely counterfeit treasure in his hands ! Woe to him, too, if, going to that
land, he forgets those who sent him and spends his
time there in selfish enjoyment of the delights of
knowledge ! Woe to him if he does not week by
week return laden, and ever more richly laden, and

saying, Yes, brothers, I have been to that land ; and it is a land of light and peace and nobleness : but I have never forgotten you and your needs and the dear bonds of brotherhood ; and look, I have brought back this, and this, and this : take them to gladden and purify your life !

I esteem it one of the chief rewards of our profession, that it makes us respect our fellow-men. It makes us continually think of even the most degraded of them as immortal souls, with magnificent undeveloped possibilities in them—as possible sons of God, and brethren of Christ, and heirs of heaven. Some men, by their profession, are continually tempted to take low views of human nature. But we are forced to think worthily of it. A minister is no minister who does not see wonder in the child in the cradle and in the peasant in the field—relations with all time behind and before, and all eternity above and beneath. Not but that we see the seamy side too— the depths as well as the heights. We get glimpses of the awful sin of the heart ; we are made to feel the force of corrupt nature's mere inert resistance to good influences ; we have to feel the pain of the slowness of the movement of goodness, as perhaps no other men do. Yet love and undying faith in the value of the soul and hope for all men are the mainsprings of our activity.

For the end we always aim at is to save those who hear us. Think what that is! What a magnificent life work! It is to fight against sin, to destroy the works of the devil, to make human souls gentle, noble and godlike, to help on the progress of the world, to sow the seed of the future, to prepare the population of heaven, to be fellow-sufferers and fellow-workers with Christ, and to glorify God.

This is your work; and the only true measure of ministerial success is how many souls you save —save in every sense—in the sense of regeneration, and sanctification, and redemption.

THE END.

represents an extensive sphere of experience and duty, the author follows our Lord through them one after another, and shows us how He conducted Himself in each. The pages are beacon lights, guiding us in our life's journey; and no one can peruse them without being profoundly impressed with the wealth of the Gospels in counsels of perfection as to human conduct."—*Christian.*

"Will sustain the author's already high reputation as a thinker and a literary artist. To our mind the strongest chapters are those which belong to Mr. Stalker's original idea in writing his book—'Christ as a Preacher' and 'Christ as a Teacher.' It is hardly possible to commend too highly the work which the author has bestowed on these two themes. It is a volume alive with interest."—*Glasgow Herald.*

"It is the finest piece of devotional literature the Church has received for many a year. The freshness of thought, lucidity of style, reverence of spirit, and direct practical tone, will make it prized as a book for quiet hours."—*Christian Leader.*

"The study of the methods and matter of Christ's teaching, which he has continued from his *Life of Christ*, is even fresher and better than anything in that brilliant little book."—*Scots Observer.*

"It is not easy to speak of Mr. Stalker's book without exaggeration, and we are not surprised that some of our contemporaries have pronounced it superior to his *Life of Christ*. A more suggestive book for the Christian teacher we have not read for years. It abounds in new and true ideas, always clearly, often strikingly expressed."—*Methodist Recorder.*

"His previous books on the *Life of Christ* and the *Life of St. Paul* have had a great vogue here and abroad. But this is a greater book than either, and fitted to exercise a still wider influence. We need not dwell on the many-sided culture manifested everywhere, or the author's remarkable literary gifts, shown especially in pregnant aphorisms and vivid descriptions. His thoughts are always arranged and expressed with exquisite order and lucidity, and he throws an occasional plummet marvellously far into the depths of his subject. But the power and beauty and life of the work mainly come from this, that the author has been in living contact with Christ and man."—*British Weekly.*

Other SGCB Classic Reprints

Biblical and Theological Studies by the faculty of Princeton Seminary was published in 1912 at the one-hundredth anniversary of the school. Warfield, Vos, Machen, Allis, Patton, Armstrong and many others wrote articles touching upon a wide variety of subjects. David B. Calhoun has written a new introduction and biographical sketches for each writer.

A History of Preaching by Edwin Charles Dargan is a two volume hardcover set that is the standard work of its kind in the field of Homiletics. Every pastor, student and teacher of religion should own it.

Homiletics and Pastoral Theology by W.G.T. Shedd expounds almost every aspect of preaching, analyzing its nature, outlining the main features which should characterize powerful preaching. The second part is devoted to the vital subject of Pastoral Theology.

The Power of God unto Salvation by B.B. Warfield is the hundredth anniversary edition of Warfield's first volume of sermons. This volume includes a warmly written Preface by *Sinclair Ferguson*, and an Appendix of Four Hymns and Eleven Religious Poems written by Warfield.

Christ in Song: Hymns of Immanuel from all ages by Philip Schaff drew forth the following high praise from Charles Hodge, *"After all, apart from the Bible, the best antidote to all these false theories of the person and work of Christ, is such a book as Dr. Schaff's 'Christ in Song.'"*

The Shorter Catechism Illustrated, from Christian Biography and History by John Whitercoss first appeared in 1828 and passed through many editions. It last appeared in 1968 by Banner of Truth.

Ichabod Spencer's LIFE & SERMONS in 3 volumes. The author of the marvelous volumes "A Pastor's Sketches" will speak directly to your heart in these soul-stirring sermons. Volume one contains a sketch of Spencer and 20 practical sermons. Volume two contains 25 doctrinal sermons, and volume three contains 26 sacramental sermons.

First Things by Gardiner Spring is a two volume set that brings before our minds the foundation upon which all life is built, as recorded in the opening chapters of Genesis.

The Church Member's Guide by John Angell James was once the most popular book in both the UK and the USA for instructing Christian's in their privileges and responsibilities as members of the body of Christ.

Young Lady's Guide: to the Harmonious Development of Christian Character by Harvey Newcomb sets forth the biblical foundation needed for a young lady to grow to Christian womanhood.

Call us toll free **1-877-666-9469**
E-mail us at **sgcb@charter.net**
Visit us on the web at **solid-ground-books.com**

Printed in the United States
152873LV00001B/3/A